Book One: Heartbreak

From Survival to Success

"An unflinchingly honest story of unimaginable hardship which speaks to everyone about the power of hope in not just surviving, but in succeeding."

Richard Moriarty - The Sun

"An immensely moving, inspirational and unforgettable journey of survival through heartbreak. A must-read."

Chris Riches - Daily Express

The Fate We Make

Book One: Heartbreak

From Survival to Success

by

Simone Warren

The Fate We Make© Copyright 2023 Simone Warren

Copyright notice: All rights reserved under the International and Pan-American Copyright Conventions. No part of this book may be reproduced or transmitted in any form or by any means, electronic or mechanical, including photocopying and recording, or by any information storage and retrieval system, without permission in writing from publisher.

This book is a memoir. It reflects the author's present recollections of experiences over time. Some names and characteristics have been changed, some events have been compressed, and some dialogue has been recreated. For privacy reasons, some names, locations, and dates may have been changed.

Warning: the unauthorized reproduction or distribution of this copyrighted work is illegal. Criminal copyright infringement, including infringement without monetary gain, is investigated by the FBI and is punishable by up to 5 years in prison and a fine of $250,000.

For more information, email simone@thefatewemake.com

9781739369408 – Limited Edition Hardback
9781739369415 – Paperback
9781739369422 - eBook

Author photo by Sam Furlong.

All other photographs © the author.

https://thefatewemake.com/

For Doug, Marc, Joe and Samaria.

Always.

Foreword

Mai diam (Don't be silent)

I am Lee Kin Mun, better known as mrbrown, the Blogfather of Singapore. Since 1997, I have been up to mischief online since the dawn of Singapore's internet, writing satire, penning silly songs, making comedy podcasts like the mrbrown show (one of the earliest and longest running podcasts in Singapore) and producing online videos as Kim Huat, Singapore's Number One complainer.

I first met Simone when we were sixteen, fresh out of the O Levels. We were both on a Humanities programme in Hwa Chong Junior College in Singapore, preparing to do our A Levels for the next two years.

The Promsho programme, as the Humanities programme was also called, and the Junior College I attended, were considered an elite scheme in an elite school, where the students were destined for great things like senior government positions and scholarships to prestigious overseas universities like Oxford and Cambridge. Many of my peers went on to become lawyers, bankers, judges and senior civil servants.

Being the class clown and general daydreamer, I was not destined for those pathways.

But I had a wonderful time studying there, with all these fun and brainy people. And to this day, we still meet as a class, in our fifties. These friendships have lasted decades.

In school, Simone was like a sister to me. We hung out together with a small group of friends, enjoying a game of carrom, exchanging views on music, drama and theatre. Simone recently reminded me of the time we came in second place for a talent contest in school, singing a duet of "Through the Eyes of Love", the theme song of movie, Ice Castles.

Ice Castles is an inspirational story about an Olympic ice skater, who battled her way back from poor relationship choices and hardship to overcome tragedy and succeed once more, with love and support from her true love and family. Now that I think about it, it is a story not unlike Simone's, which she tells with unflinching honesty in 'The Fate We Make' trilogy of memoirs.

Even though we have been friends since our youth, and into adulthood, I never knew how hard her life was. Sure, I knew some details as we grew up, like when she got married, and then remarried, and had kids, but not some of the darker days of her life. Being Asians, we tend not to share private matters, especially when it comes to family matters.

Saving face was very much part of our conservative Asian upbringing, and while things are more open now for my children's generation, back then it was common to avoid shame and embarrassment at all costs, lest we bring disrepute to our family.

In 1989, Simone moved away to study, live and work abroad, and we stayed connected sporadically until the advent of social media.

When she asked me to write the foreword to Book One: Heartbreak, I felt both honoured and mortified. Why me? How would I convey the essence of the book and explain why I think people should read it? And to think that I just found out about this huge chapter of her life too!

When we were growing up, there was no such thing as mental health awareness, and women in our traditional Asian society had to deal with difficult questions like who do you marry, when do you have children, how do you cope with the pressures of both being a modern educated working woman while living up to the expectations of being a wife and mother.

The World Health Organisation cites suicide as the leading cause of deaths worldwide — this has risen to 800,000 in 2022 from 703,000 in 2019. And for every suicide death, there are many unrecorded attempts. How we deal with adversity, abuse and failure, without succumbing to taking our lives, is a constant challenge in our complex, ever-changing world.

So, this is why I really think you should read my friend's autobiography. Simone shares her life story and those of her female relatives so candidly, that you feel like you are re-living their experiences, getting an inside track into how they thought and felt at the time. She takes us back to the late 1800s, when arranged marriages were commonplace and where a measure of a Chinese woman's beauty was the size of her bound feet. It is an emotional rollercoaster ride. At some points, events are so shocking, I had to remember to breathe.

But I could not put this book down. Not only because I know the author, Simone, but because I had to see how she managed to not just survive but overcome all of this and thrive.

It pains me that Simone had to suffer in silence as a teenager in 1987, unable to even tell her close friends why she suddenly disappeared from school just before the A Levels. I admire her for moving past those dark days of depression, for sharing her story so vividly and with such openness, urging us to always be kind because so many of us hide so much behind a brave smile.

'The Fate We Make' memoirs will shock you, move you, inspire you, and maybe even make you cry. Ultimately, you will feel encouraged to persevere through tough times, realise the importance of self-love and find out how to remain hopeful when faced with adversity.

I think her story is more relevant than ever, even in this post-social media world. If anything, the social pressures are bigger, the need to conform weighs heavier, and the personal stakes are higher than ever. We will do well to learn from Simone's story of struggle in the face of overwhelming odds.

If there is only one memoir you read this year, make it this one.

Signed,

Lee Kin Mun
    a.k.a. mrbrown
    Singapore, May 2023

Simone and me at London's King Cross St Pancras station, taken on 8th November 2017

Contents

Introduction	1
Part One: Me, Singapore (1901 to 1987)	5
Prelude	9
Chapter 1: First Lessons on Life and Love	12
Chapter 2: A Legacy of Love Stories	22
Chapter 3: Love in Real Life	43
Interlude 1	75
Part Two: Me, Singapore & UK (1988 to 1994)	77
Chapter 4: Just Geography	79
Chapter 5: The Lost Years	90
Interlude 2	107
Chapter 6: How to Save a Life	109
Interlude 3	119
Part Three: Me, UK & New Zealand (1995 to 2006)	121
Chapter 7: Happiness is just a Pipe Dream	123
Interlude 4	139
Chapter 8: Daring to Dream Again	141
Chapter 9: Muted	156
Interlude 5	163

Part Four: Me, UK (2006 to 2022) — 165
    Chapter 10: Time to Move On — 167
    Chapter 11: Should I Stay or Should I Go — 174

Interlude 6 — 189

    Chapter 12: Prince Charming — 191

Interlude 7 — 205

Part Five: You & Me, Singapore & UK (1987, 2022) — 207
    Choices — 209

Interlude 8 — 215

    Consequences — 217
    Chaos — 231

Interlude 9 — 245

Postlude (December 2022) — 247

Acknowledgements — 253
About the Author — 255

Introduction

THIS IS MY memoir — a very personal story of families and fate. I feel strongly that family is the cornerstone of every person's life. My complex Chinese family laid the foundations for my life before I was born, before I was even a twinkle in my parents' eyes. My ancestors' lived experiences over the centuries shaped the choices they made, with each successive generation creating consequences which would sometimes be fortunate, but at other times so traumatic, they became a stronghold of secret heirlooms, never talked about in public but spoken of in private from mother to child, to pass on life lessons from our family's rich heritage.

I decided in December 2022 to unveil some of these secrets, initially to find someone I thought I had lost forever; then ultimately, to share my struggles and those of the strong women in my maternal family which shaped my thinking, decisions and life journey. I am sharing our stories to help you, in case you too are struggling with the hand fate has dealt you. This book comes with a health warning — it is an honest and harrowing account of true events. It covers many taboo topics including addiction, abortion, adoption, infertility, loss, grief, mental health issues, dysfunctional families, infidelity, rape, abuse and violence.

I hope that you will take heart from reading my story. I hope you will start believing that it is possible to survive through unimaginable adversity, through decades of intergenerational trauma, if we can just find the balance between self-love and selflessness, with the help of family and friends. I hope you

will find it within yourself to always be kind because no one knows the sadness that hides behind someone's smile. I hope you will make better choices than I did and find love and happiness more easily than me.

To help western readers understand my eastern mindset, I'll try to summarise the historical context. Singapore became a British colony in February 1819 due to its strategic trading position for the British East India Company. Sir Stamford Raffles, then Lieutenant Governor of the British colony in Bencoolen, oversaw the expansion of the island's population from 1,000 to over 100,000 in just two years, bringing in mainly male workers from Malaya, China, India and other parts of Asia to work at rubber plantations and tin mines. More than half of the immigrants were from China. My maternal great-grandfather (grandfather's dad) was one of those migrant workers, arriving in Singapore in 1888 aged twelve, working hard to send money back to his impoverished family in the Fujian province of China.

My great-grandmother (left), prized for her beauty and tiny two-inch bound feet, joined him eight years later through a marriage arranged by my great-great-grandparents. My great-grandfather managed to amass a small fortune through property investments, and by the time my grandfather (Ang Ban Chuan) was born in 1899, the Angs owned most of the land in the Great World area in Singapore.

The first Catholic missionaries arrived in 1871 but the local Malays, Chinese and Indians mainly stuck to their own faiths. My family were devout Taoists and firm believers in fate, but they also believed that you make your own fate by the choices you take. My great-grandfather, though wealthy with an extensive property portfolio, was a stickler for tradition. This meant that my grandfather, his two brothers and their families, all lived with my great-grandparents in the same house as the other wives and concubines of my great-grandfather. My grandmother's family were slightly different because she was the only child of her father's first wife, a Singapore-born Chinese girl (known as Peranakan[1] because they were Straits-born[2] Chinese). My maternal great-grandfather only took a second wife after his first wife failed to produce a male heir to perpetuate the family name. My grandmother and her half-brother lived in the same house along with their mothers. Such was the nature of the traditional Chinese nuclear family. And so it continued through to my early childhood.

Singapore is a melting pot of multiracial cultures blending with British culture. We had to learn to co-exist in such a small space (the entire island could fit comfortably within Greater London's boundaries), to live in harmony despite so much cultural diversity. There were many race riots and violent clashes during the 1960s, the decade when I was born. In many ways, the superior master-servant mentality towards all immigrants (particularly those from China) was best summed up in the sign outside the exclusive Tanglin Club for British expatriates — *No dogs or Chinese*. By the time Singapore gained independence from Britain in 1965, most Singaporean Chinese were able to speak their own dialect, maybe some Malay, with English becoming their first language. All Singaporeans are able to speak Singlish[3] — a blend of English, Chinese dialects, Malay and Indian mother tongues. Polygamy is now illegal unless you are a practising Muslim.

Singapore's population growth (100,000 in 1821 to 2m in 1969 to 5.64m in 2022), economic rags-to-riches story, and

---

1. Peranakan: a person of mixed Chinese and Malay/Indonesian heritage. Many Singapore Peranakans trace their origins to 15th-century Malacca, where their ancestors were thought to be Chinese traders who married local women.

2. Straits-born: born in the Malacca Straits.

3. Singlish: Singaporean English, similar to slang.

rapid cultural change are nothing short of astounding. The Lion City's radical transformation was engineered by PM Harry Lee Kuan Yew who graduated with a double first in Law from the University of Cambridge. As one of the founding fathers of our island nation, he established a one-party political framework that brought together the best of eastern socialism and western capitalism with a relentless focus on developing Singapore's most precious asset: its people.

One thing is clear though — however westernised the average Singaporean Chinese person appears to be, we remain rooted in the traditions, values and beliefs of ancient China from as far back as 296 BC. We still believe in sacrificing self-interest for the greater good, always put family first, and eschew freedom of speech, preferring instead to suffer in silence. As my Scottish husband often says, "It is better to stay silent and look a fool than to open your mouth and confirm it". If there is one thing to bear in mind as you read on, this would be it. Most Singaporeans will do almost anything to 'save face'. I am not one of them.

Three Generations of Singapore-born Chinese on my grandmother's 80th birthday in 1981. I am in the back row, far right, aged 11.

Part One
Me, Singapore
(1901 to 1987)

"It is not our abilities that show what we truly are.
It is our choices."

Albus Dumbledore,
'Harry Potter and the Chamber of Secrets' movie 2002,
based on the book by J.K. Rowling

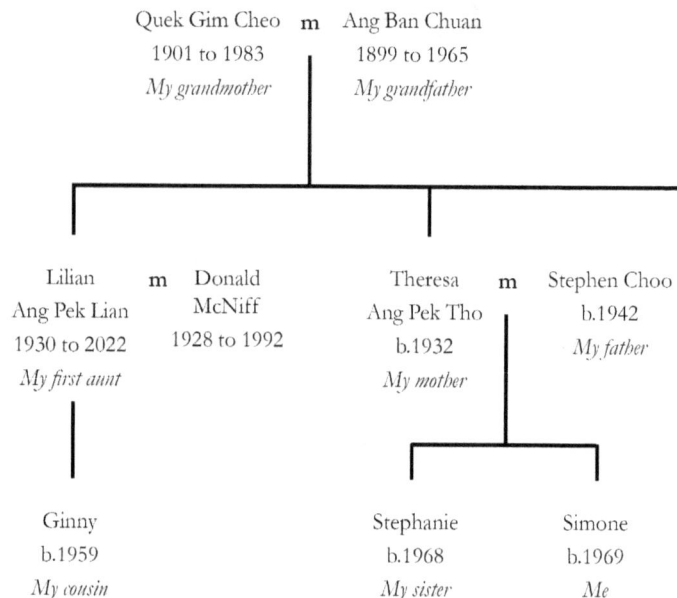

My Family Tree

Philomena **m** Eng Swee Tan
Ang Pek Eng　　b.1933
b.1934
My third aunt

Laurence
Ang Tiong Huat
1935 to 2020
My uncle

Rosalind
b.1968
My adopted cousin

Prelude

AGED SEVENTEEN, I have a choice to make. While other girls my age are deciding which outfit to wear to their weekend parties, if natural or smoky eyes would allure more, to dance in kitten heels or kinky boots, I face the impossibly difficult decision of whether I should end my unborn baby's life.

I stare blankly out of my bedroom window at the kidney-shaped swimming pool of our noveau-riche District 10 condo in Bukit Timah, trying to make sense of the situation. My Inner Conscience is doing a decent job of drowning out the clamorous chants of her cousin Common Sense. Their internal debate rages on endlessly like a discordant cacophony of jarring voices, each shouting louder and competing to be heard. My sister stands helplessly by my side, also at a loss about what to do next, but trying her best to support.

This is unfamiliar territory for both of us, the hardest decision we've taken so far in our lives is which subjects to choose for study at A-Level. I choke back the wave of panic as I struggle to breathe, sweat beading on my brow even though the air-conditioner is on, my chest heavy with the weight of my dilemma.

Trying desperately to regain some semblance of balance, I make a list, like so:

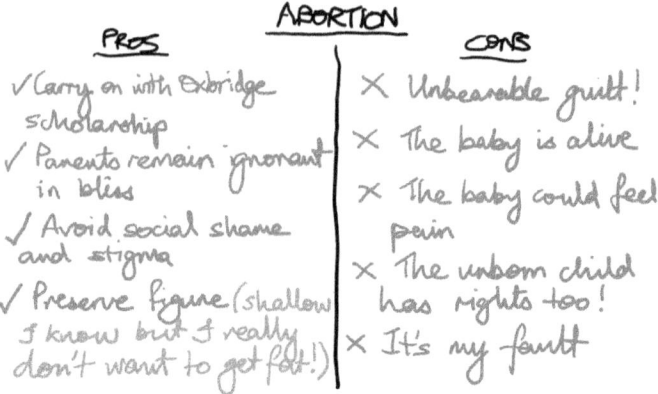

This list lengthens as I agonise over every single conflicting perspective. I imagine every potential outcome. I feel sick to my stomach as a kaleidoscope of bloodstained abortion images projects across my mind's eye, and I can actually feel the excruciating pain of my baby as it is torn limb from limb, then forcibly removed via the Dilation & Curettage procedure. It puts my teeth and everything else on edge. I recall watching a graphically gruesome video depicting what happens during an abortion by the Pro-Life Society at the Catholic primary school I'd attended only six years ago. I shudder with guilt at the thought of inflicting such pain and suffering on an innocent child.

Almost immediately switching scenes to escape the horror, I picture myself moving on from Babyblip to successfully complete my A-level and Oxbridge entrance exams; I see myself laughing while enjoying a punt on the River Cam and dining in ridiculous robes alongside newfound friends, soaking up knowledge and opportunity.

In an alternative universe, I'm an unmarried mum shunned by everyone except my parents, living a shameful existence with a bastard child, all hopes and dreams of studying and living abroad dashed forever. Or perhaps the slightly less unappealing prospect of marrying Adam, my boyfriend of four years, and trying our best to bring up our child without any support from my parents, who I feel sure would instantly disown me. Mentally, I travel down that path, desperately trying to picture a positive outcome, but all I can see is another child growing up unhappily in another broken home with disillusioned parents who had married in haste and were repenting at leisure. All potential paths appear bleak and desolate.

I grapple with crippling guilt, feeling that I am damned no matter what I decide to do. I'm completely convinced that my soul will burn in hell for evermore, bypassing purgatory altogether, and all because I had chosen not to resist the guilty and forbidden intimacies of pre-marital sex. More than anything, I want desperately for my fairy godmother to wave her magic wand and erase everything that has led to this painful point in my life. I just want someone to hold me and lie to me shamelessly that everything will work out well, and we will all live happily ever after.

But I'm on my own. Fairy godmothers don't exist anywhere other than our imaginations. No matter how much I pinch myself, I'm still stuck in this waking nightmare. Adam isn't with me because he's in the army camp at Pulau Tekong Besar halfway through National Service. Even if he wasn't away doing his NS, our unsanctioned relationship means we've been sneaking around in secret since we first met when I was thirteen. I can't confide in any of my friends at school because I'm afraid that my family will become the subject of the relentless rumour mill; also I'm almost always the confidante, never the confider. My parents are too busy with work and too caught up with the crazy business of keeping up with the Tans[4] to be there for me. More than anything, I feel deeply ashamed to find myself mired in the dire predicament my Mum has warned me about, for as long as I can remember.

I feel very much alone.

---

4. Keeping up with the Tans: the Singapore equivalent of Keeping Up with the Joneses, Tan being the most common Chinese surname in Singapore.

Stubbornly Mute

I WAS NOTORIOUSLY silent till I turned three. Maybe it was because I never needed to say anything until then. Or perhaps no one was around to hear my first words, or they didn't remember. In any case, there were numerous trips to the doctor to check my vocal cords and then my hearing, because my parents were convinced that I was a deaf-mute or maybe just mute. The doctors told my Mum not to worry, "Mai-kia[5] Mrs Choo, everything is normal lah[6]! She can speak if she wants to, so maybe she just doesn't want to, leh[7]?"

"Kam-sia[8] doctor! My eldest started speaking at eighteen

---

5. Mai-kia: Hokkien word meaning 'don't be scared'.

6. Lah: A particle used at the end of a sentence to express finality or frustration/strong feelings.

7. Leh: A particle used at the end of a sentence to express feelings, less certain than Lah.

8. Kam-sia: Thank You in Hokkien.

months so we're worried about Simone because all the other children who are same age, are already speaking hor[9]. We don't want her to fall behind when she goes to school!"

Apparently, I didn't even speak when my older sister Stephanie was kidnapped. I was two at the time and clearly understood what was being said, but I responded by either doing what was asked of me or gesturing to communicate my thoughts. The whole family on both sides descended upon my mama's[10] multi-generational family home in Katong, as did the police and local reporters. When one of my uncles asked me if I knew where my che-che[11] was, I shook my head. When they asked me what she was doing, I mimed, by placing both palms under my tilted head and squeezing my eyes shut, that she was sleeping.

This stressful situation was the straw that broke the camel's back. Suddenly, a lifetime of unuttered, pent-up grievances smashed through the fragile emotional dam shoring up my mum's

---

9. Hor: Emphasises the need for the listener to acknowledge something.

10. Mama: Grandmother, can be maternal or paternal.

11. Che-che: older sister.

reticence as a dutiful daughter-in-law, washing away all civility and tolerance. It became Us (my mum's family) vs Them (my pa's family). My mum had committed to memory all the wrongdoings of my kongkong[12], the festering seeds of resentment bearing fruit as soon as he started interfering in the police investigation. When my khookhoo[13] asked politely if he could just let the police get on with it, my kongkong started swearing at him and threatened violence. Said police had to intervene to break up the potential fight.

The floodgates opened immediately. My mum blamed my grandfather for a multitude of sins including the death of his first wife who had died while giving birth to the last of their four children. For infecting my paternal mama (his second wife) and my pa (when he was a new-born) with syphilis from his liaisons with ladies of the night after the death of his first wife. For punishing my cheeky pa, aged nine, when he stole some mangoes from the English naval base at Sembawang by caning him, then making him stand barefoot on hot cockle shells at midday in the tropical heat. For refusing to help his son (my pa) and his daughter-in-law financially when they were struggling to make ends meet, instead demanding a monthly 'allowance' to demonstrate filial piety ... enough was enough! My kongkong left that day after angry words were exchanged and I never saw him again.

After five stretched days, my sister was finally traced to an address in Malaysia. My mum almost lost her mind from worry and guilt because it turned out that the kidnappers had colluded with a couple who lodged in the flat we shared with my pa's half-brother (nicknamed Devil Joe by my mum and not in a fond way). The female lodger met Steph on her short walk home from the school bus and persuaded her to go see 'Mummy' in her office. Even aged four, Steph would never have gone with a stranger because my mum had always warned us about the

---

12. Kongkong: grandfather, maternal or paternal

13. Khookhoo: uncle (mother's brother)

dangers of dealing with people we didn't know, particularly men.

Following Steph's safe return, my mum issued an edict to my pa – he could still have contact with his family but as far as she, Steph and I were concerned, my paternal family was now 'excommunicated' from our family church. She also refused to set foot in the shared flat ever again, blaming my sister's misfortune on bad Feng Shui and Devil Joe practising Gong Tao[14] in the flat with his sacrificial offerings to Taoist deities in foul-smelling jars at a makeshift altar. She insisted on moving us all into one of the rooms at Mama's Marshall Road mansion, so we could live with her sisters, brother and their families, sharing domestic help and receiving support from Mama, the matriarch of our family. My mum had married beneath her social class. The Angs (her father's family) were wealthy until her father and uncles sold off all the assets accumulated by their China-born father in colonial Singapore.

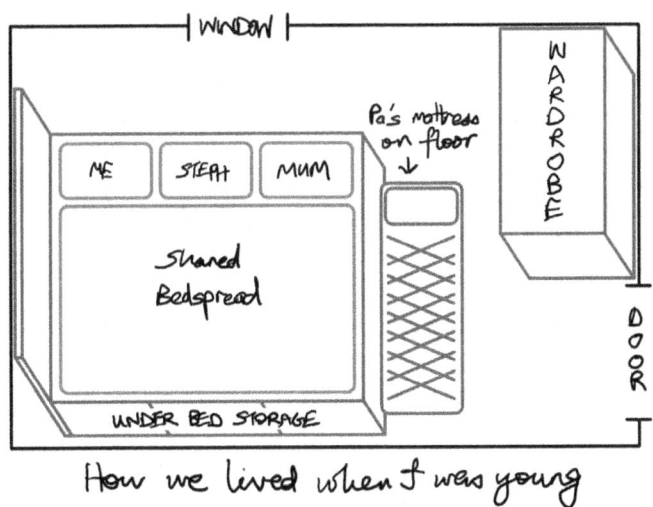

How we lived when I was young

Some of my earliest memories involved listening to the raised voices of my parents when they thought we were sleeping,

---

14. Gong Tao: black magic/voodoo.

especially after my pa had come home full of Dutch courage from entertaining customers. We would lie motionless as my mum got under the covers at the end of the bed, looking down on my pa as he rolled onto his mattress with a grumbling grunt. They always started with furious whispers, but by the end of their well-practised sermons, their protestations were as passionate and agitated as gospel preachers' cadenced voices evangelising to their flocks. However, the same old litanies about family feuds never seemed to enlighten either Mum or Pa to the other's point of view, no matter how many times they were recited! They would eventually turn their backs to each other, after exhausting every counter-argument, to catch some shut-eye before our 5am starts. Our family life was a permanent state of disagreement with zero to no chance of resolution or compromise. Our family motto was 'Just tahan[15], cover up and carry on'.

Indeed, my early life was extremely eventful and full of the drama, colour, and noise that are part and parcel of an extended Chinese family, so maybe being silent for three years was just my way of blending in to avoid drawing undue attention to myself. After all, I'd always been told by my elders that children should be seen, not heard. Many prayers were murmured fervently on bended knees at Sunday mass beseeching God, Jesus, Mary, Joseph and any Saint who would listen to make me speak so I wouldn't struggle at school. It wasn't until I was under threat of a caning from my Pa for misbehaving, that I obliged with a fully formed, grammatically perfect answer to his rhetorical question:

"Mone[16], why are you so NAUGHTY?" his angry-red face loomed over me with his hand poised and ready to strike.

"Because I was born naughty." Flabbergasted, caning forgotten, he picked me up in glee and ran through the house celebrating my newfound voice.

Years later, I'm told I'm Little Miss Chatterbox. Oh the irony.

---

15. Tahan: Malay word meaning bear, tolerate or handle stress, trouble, burdens.

16. Mone: my family's nickname for me, the shortened version of Simone.

A Logical Dreamer

I USED TO wander from bedroom to bedroom during the weekends when we were all at home. My favourite pastime was lying in between each Auntie and Uncle having random conversations about anything and everything. My sar-teoh[17] was a schoolteacher. It was he who discovered, when I was able to solve a Maths puzzle that even six-year-olds found hard, that I have a highly logical mind. Up till then, I'd been written off as the less smart daughter especially when I didn't speak, so Sar-teoh's assessment elevated me into the spotlight aged three. My parents' attention piqued, they ensured I was sent to the top Catholic Kindergarten, Primary and Secondary schools. My mum spent most days reminding us how important education was, "Girls, it's your passport to independence and financial freedom. Don't depend on a man if you can help it!"

We were not allowed to go out on our own. My mum was over forty by now and had tragically miscarried two boys in the second trimester so we, her precious daughters, needed to be wrapped up in cotton wool for our own protection. My sister, still traumatised by her kidnapping experience, obeyed the rules religiously, but I learned when and how I could bend them without getting caught. Steph developed compulsive behaviours like scrubbing her hands raw several times every hour, and checking to see if she had switched off appliances and lights a set number of times, an omen of more troubled times to come in later years. My only foible was sleepwalking, which sounds innocuous, but had painful consequences when I banged my head down on the table fan rather than the pillow, turned our shared bedroom into a bloody crime scene, and had to have my chin stitched up without anaesthetic at A&E. Coincidentally, I began sleepwalking shortly after the discovery of my academic potential.

We never went on foreign holidays, the most exotic holiday being a day-trip to Sentosa, again due to my mum's paranoiac

---

17. Sar-teoh: husband of my third aunt.

fear that we would come to serious harm if we strayed too far from home. I soon discovered that I could travel using my mind through reading, and devoured books as other children devoured sweets, my imagination taking me to far flung, exotic places because my body couldn't. By the time I was seven or eight, I was reading Austen and the Brontës; I used to pretend I was Elizabeth Bennet or Jane Eyre, not Catherine though, because her relationship with Heathcliff seemed more like possession than love. I developed a strong interest in theatre, dramatic arts and music, and began formal courses in music, speech and drama. My ability to do well in science and mathematics continued but it was the humanities subjects that fired my imagination and made me want to travel the world. By the time I was twelve, I told my mum that my ambition was to be a Volunteer Support Officer in Africa; aghast, she said it was life-threatening and told me to think of something else! When I said I wanted to be a nurse, she told me to "be a doctor, you'll earn much more!". After this point, I stopped sharing my thoughts and dreams. I knew she wouldn't understand because her life's ambition was to ensure her daughters got the university education she had never had, and she wanted more than anything for us to make something of ourselves.

I dreamt about learning to ride a bike after my mum deemed it too dangerous. My pa was always travelling and thus too busy to teach me! When they were both at work, I used to wander around our condominium estate making friends with other young people, some of the same age (twelve) and others in their late teens or early twenties. I was the 'ball girl' during their friendly tennis matches and after months of post-match conversations, one of my 'big brothers' called me precocious, explaining with a chuckle that I was twelve going on twenty-two. I had a secret crush on my neighbour's older brother who was at just the perfect age (sixteen) to be adored from a distance. We used to bump into each other regularly but despite his cheerful "Hi, how are you?", my tongue refused to cooperate as if I were a toddler once more, so all I could do was wave back, smiling shyly as he cycled past on his mountain bike.

Embarrassed, I borrowed my friend's bike and practised until I felt confident enough to go for a ride around the estate. All went well until the day we decided to cycle to the East Coast beach which involved navigating hairpin bends in the underpass beneath the East Coast Parkway. I was too inexperienced to brake in time for the turn after hurtling down the underpass ramp and crashed headfirst into the concrete wall. When I regained consciousness, I vaguely remembered being lifted onto a stretcher and transported somewhere with sirens blaring. My head was pounding even harder when I heard my mum shouting at me moments later, "You see what happens when you don't listen to me. I told you it was dangerous but you went ahead anyway! Well, you made your bed so you can lie in it!". She turned on her heel and marched out of the ward without a backward glance, leaving my pa to deal with the doctors and me. I remember being violently sick with a severe concussion and a mango-sized bump on my forehead, but when I returned home, my mum refused to talk to me for three days until I got down on my knees, begged for forgiveness and promised never to do it again. I had to care for myself until then.

Meanwhile, my kwai[18] sister never got up to any mischief. I admired and secretly envied how Steph maintained her laser focus on studying, how she managed to block out all distractions. Effectively grounded after the bike accident, I only did the bare minimum where homework was concerned, preferring to use my spare time reading books outside of the prescribed curriculum or listening to music — the vinyls my cousin had left behind when she emigrated to the UK with my tua ee[19]. Music was my way of escaping the hum-drumness of everyday life, it made me feel alive and connected to my hopes and dreams. But there was no room for these feelings or for such frivolity

---

18. Kwai: Adjective: good (as in goody-two-shoes).

19. Tua ee: Big auntie (first aunt).

in the Singaporean education system. All of us were 'streamed' with ruthless precision — we regularly took exams from ages six to sixteen to determine which stream we would be placed in. Steph and I, spurred on by our classic Asian Tiger mum, were always in the top stream, swimming furiously against the other hapless fish and competing for top results, kiasu[20] about being the under-achievers.

I remember baulking at the relentless pressure once aged eight, when I deliberately didn't revise for a Maths test and failed spectacularly. I tried to think of excuses for not handing in my daily progress report to my mum that day, but failed miserably. So with shaky hands and voice, I placed it in front of her after dinner. Surprisingly, she appeared quite calm and said very little, apart from asking me why I didn't know my times tables, then telling me to get ready for bed. Later when we were all in bed, Mum produced a cane and proceeded to test me on my times tables. Every time I got an answer wrong, she leaned over Steph and whacked me hard across the shins until I got it right. Eventually, we got to 7x8 which I repeatedly got wrong. By now, I was bawling my eyes out but Mum kept going until finally, close to 1am, I muttered feebly, "Fifty-six". Satisfied, she turned over and went to sleep. I lay awake for ages, feeling bad for doing what I wanted rather than what was expected of me, for not trying harder and for not getting things right first time. I vowed never to make the same mistake again.

My parents were proud as punch the day Steph was awarded the Public Services Commission Humanities scholarship and started at Hwa Chong Junior College. It was inevitable that they expected the same from me; I didn't dare disappoint. By 1986, after years of scrimping, saving and sacrifice, they had reached the pinnacle of parental bragging rights — two girls in HCJC on the Oxbridge Humanities scholarship programme. Every small achievement and performance along the way was just another small step on the journey to fulfil this lifelong dream. I

---

20. Kiasu: Singlish for 'scared to lose'.

remember singing, acting and performing for my parents' friends at Chinese New Year, at family gatherings and later on the school stage to hundreds of strangers, cast in lead roles and firmly in the spotlight, my name up in lights!

My sister imploded first — before her exams, she just lost it and had a mini nervous breakdown. She eventually scraped together the grades she needed to get into uni but only as a privately funded international student. My parents had to borrow money from rich family and friends to fund her education.

As for me, after a fairly uneventful life following the bike accident, I was all set to reverse the fall from grace — until I fell pregnant. I dreaded disappointing my parents because I knew they had pinned all hopes on me after Steph's hiccup; they had all these ambitions and dreams for me to achieve, hoping that wealth would follow soon after success. I spent most of my childhood and youth anxiously trying to achieve their dreams, to make them proud, to repay them for the sacrifices they had made over the years, to live up to the Singaporean Dream of the four C's — Career, Cash, Condo, Car. But all I ever dreamt about and longed for was love and happiness.

Sounds so simple, doesn't it?

Except that experience has taught me how elusive they really are.

Chapter 2
A Legacy of Love Stories

In the voices of my female forebears

My Maternal Grandmother: Cecilia (Quek Gim Cheo, DOB 27 September 1901)

"GIM CHEO, WAKE up. We need to get you ready to meet Ban Chuan. You must look beautiful so your pa can agree the marriage with his parents."

I groan inwardly as I reluctantly drag myself out of bed. It's five o'clock in the morning and all I want to do is sleep, not be poked, prodded and prepared for a meeting with my future husband. But as the only child of a rich businessman, I need to help my father secure a partnership with Ang Ban Chuan's father, one of the wealthiest self-made towkay[21] landowners in post-war Si Lat Po[22]. My Peranakan mother and six maids spare no effort in preparing me for the momentous occasion, unfurling the gold krosang and hand-stitched sarong kebaya carefully from layers of tissue wrap. Four hours later, buffed and beautified to within an inch of my life, surrounded by our parents, numerous aunties, uncles and a multitude of waiting servants, we meet.

I know you, whispers a voice from deep within my heart, as a deafening silence drowns out the hubbub around me. Ang Ban Chuan smiles softly in reply with the same sense of recognition, holding my gaze with equal intensity and passion. Four

---

21. Towkay: from Malay meaning boss.
22. Si Lat Po: Old Chinese name for Singapore (coined in the 1900s).

Gim Cheo, aged
39 and 55,
in 1940 and 1956

weeks later, we're married and the union of two of Singapore's wealthiest families, the Angs and the Queks, is complete. We are inseparable. Despite living in a mansion, we shun the tradition of separate sleeping quarters. We are together morning, noon and night, spend hours taking leisurely baths together, oblivious to the world around us. Our children are born in rapid succession, twelve over sixteen years, each looked after by their own maid. We are so desperate to be together that he breaks with tradition to sleep with me during my month of confinement after each of our sons and daughters are born.

My mother-in-law is uneasy about our obsessive closeness. Her three sons were born into wealth and have never worked a day in their life, choosing instead to sell off our family's property assets to fund their towkay lifestyles, squandering the legacy built up by my father-in-law from the age of twelve when he left China to cook for British colonists in the 1800s, so small in stature that he had to stand on a stack of wooden pallets to reach the stove. She introduces Ban Chuan to a stick-thin pei pa chai[23],

---

23. Pei pa chai: Pipa girls/sing song girls paid by the hour to play mahjong or

my polar opposite, under the pretext of playing mahjong, but with the cunning intention of encouraging him to take a second wife. My heart breaks when he finally abides with tradition even though, out of respect for me, he houses his second wife in another location.

But I have no time to grieve the death of our intimacy because my children begin to die, one by one, falling like dominoes when they succumb in quick succession to typhoid. Desperate to save them, I turn my back on Taoism and convert to Catholicism, and am christened Cecilia. I pray to God, Jesus and Mother Mary night and day, baptising each child in the hope of preventing their burial. By the time the Japanese invade Singapore in February 1942, 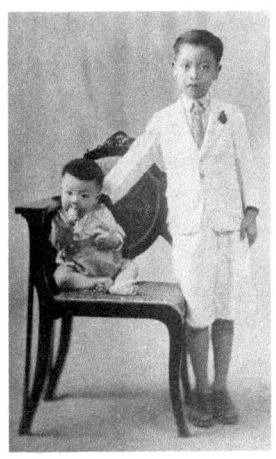 only four of my babies have survived — Lilian, Theresa, Philomena and Laurence, our youngest and only son left to carry on our family name. Our family assets have been stripped to bare bones so I have to live in the same house as the pei pa chai. Fear spreads when word begins to circulate of men being decapitated, women being raped and babies being bayoneted by the Japanese invaders. The pei pa chai refuses to leave our Stanley Street home, so I evacuate with Ban Chuan and the children to hide in a kampong house buried deep in the dense tropical jungle. The day after we flee, she is raped repeatedly but fortunately, her barren womb bears no ill fruit and they spare her life.

After the war, Ban Chuan tires of her and returns to me, helping to bring up our remaining children before his death from stomach cancer ten years later in 1965, the year Singapore gains its independence from Britain. The year before he dies, he says he is sorry for being disloyal to me with the pei pa chai,

---

prepare opium in teahouses, theatres and opium dens.

for leaving me to deal with the deaths of our eight children and the responsibilities of bringing up our surviving four, and for squandering our family fortune, forcing me to start my own business to keep a roof over our heads. He apologises profusely and asks for absolution, his eyes blazing with regret, with the same intensity and passion I saw forty-seven years ago at our first meeting when we fell in love. I forgive him because I can see that his end is near and I still love him unconditionally, giving him the peace he needs for his onward journey into the Afterlife.

My Maternal Aunt: Lilian
(Ang Pek Lian, DOB 31 August 1930)

"I COULD HAVE danced all night, I could have danced all night, and still have begged for more!", I sing to myself as I twirl and spin excitedly before the mirror, my feet itching to get going on the dance floor! I love dancing and partying at events organised by the Catholic Church, even though I'm not remotely religious. My mum is, especially as she believes that God saved me, my sisters and brother from dying of typhoid, so I try my best to observe all religious festivals and attend mass weekly. The best thing about being a practising Catholic though, is getting to meet handsome Ang-Mohs[24] at church-arranged functions.

"Lil, come over here. We'd like you to meet Arthur." My friends are standing next to a bunch of good-looking men in uniform, but it's the blonde and blue-eyed alpha male, the one they've singled out, who catches my eye.

"How do you do?" he murmurs smoothly as he bends his head to kiss my outstretched hand rather than shaking it. I feel the warmth of his breath ripple up and along my arm, and straight

---

24. Ang-Moh: Translated as 'Red Hair' - Hokkien word for a Caucasian person.

into my heart, gasping audibly at the strange sensation. He notices and a wry smile lingers on his kissable lips as he holds onto my hand just a little bit longer than decorum would expect. We talk as we dance all night long, and despite a number of other men asking to be my next dance partner, Arthur monopolises my dance card. I am genuinely interested in finding out about him, surprising myself because usually, all I'm interested in is having a dance partner who talks as little as possible. He's stationed at the British naval base and holds the rank of Captain. He is charmingly disarming and he makes me laugh. We agree to see each other again.

A few months pass and after Arthur proposes to me, we consummate our relationship. I arrange for him to meet my parents, nervous about my pa's reaction to him being an Ang-Moh. My mum is far more understanding and reassures me that there is no expectation of an arranged marriage. That misfortune will fall upon the shoulders of my youngest sibling, Laurence, because he is the male heir who's expected to perpetuate our family name and marry for fortune. I wait anxiously at the corner of Boon Tat Street and Stanley Street for an hour after the agreed time but there's still no sign of him. I feel sure I've worn away the paving stones from all my pacing back and forth in the same spot. I give him another half hour, then head towards the naval base to see if he's been delayed or involved in an accident.

The prim, blonde lady at the front office looks me up and down sympathetically when I explain who I'm looking for. Capt. Arthur Cawsey is not available, she informs me. He's away on duty and she is unable to say more. I ask when he will return, anxiety slowly creeping in, an unfamiliar stranger. She softens,

"I'm sorry dear, I really don't know. Why don't you try again in a few weeks' time?"

A few weeks later and history repeats. I trudge home despondently and tell Sa (Theresa, my younger sister) about my suspicions. I'm now convinced that Arthur only proposed so he could have his wicked way with me. Aged twenty-nine, I foolishly gave my virginity to a sweet talker who promised me love and a better life abroad. I berate myself for being so trusting, for allowing him to sweep me off my feet, for taking leave of my senses.

"Maybe he's just been held up on an exercise Lil. Don't worry, I'm sure there's a logical explanation for his absence." Sa tries to comfort me, but her words sound hollow and unconvincing, even to her.

The situation deteriorates dramatically when I realise I am pregnant. By now, I'm beginning to show and it will only be a matter of time before my mum notices because I'm very petite. Sa and I frantically try to come up with solutions — I could have an abortion at the backstreet sinsei[25] in Amoy Street, but we decide against it because we've heard horror stories of them using umbrella shafts, bicycle spokes and bamboo to dislodge the foetus; Sa suggests increasing our efforts to locate Arthur as she remains hopeful that he's just away with the Navy; eventually, we decide to look for Arthur but to also approach the newly formed Family Planning Association of Singapore for help.

Sa finds him after six weeks of asking around. He's at a dance and flirting shamelessly with a young girl who looks just like me. I walk up to him and slap him hard across his handsome, traitorous face. Laughing as he shrugs off my rage while holding onto my wrists, he pulls me outside and tries to kiss me. "Where have you been Lil? I've just come back from Malaysia and expected to see you out dancing. Why are you so angry with me?"

I'm so furious that I can't speak. Sa steps in, explains the situation and urges him to marry me soon so that the baby will be born legitimately. The colour drains from his face as the gravity of the situation sinks in. His glib answer shatters my heart into a million pieces.

"Well, how do I know it's mine? After all, you like to dance with all of us. I'm not carrying the can for someone else's child. We've had a great time Lil, but I'm going home to the old Blighty in a month so I'm afraid I won't be staying around long enough.

---

25. Sinsei: Singlish word for Doctor.

Take care of yourself though, old bean."

He strolls away casually without a care in the world.

We end up telling my mother who stays very calm. By this time, she's a successful businesswoman with a large network of connections across South East Asia. She takes charge of the situation and helps me to hide my pregnancy from my pa by sending me across the causeway to Johor Bahru where she's made arrangements for me to stay at a Catholic convent. In November 1959, I give birth on my own to a beautiful baby girl on the cold stone altar of the church because she came unexpectedly and quickly. The nuns take the baby from me because I've agreed to

give her up for adoption. I have to lie still for hours on the cold marble for fear of bleeding to death, before the doctor arrives to stitch me up five hours later. He tells me that I've suffered extensive endometrial scarring and I will not be able to bear more children in the future. The next day, they bring my daughter back. The prospective adoptive parents have decided that they would prefer a baby boy who looks less Eurasian[26].

My mum arrives to bring me home. She takes one look at her first granddaughter and falls in love with her immediately. She brings us both home and has a blazing row with my pa who is so ashamed of us that he doesn't speak a word to me until the day he dies. When Ginny is two though, my pa can't resist playing with her, and I know it's only his pride that prevents him from openly forgiving me. He says nothing but is always the first to offer me a blanket if it gets chilly or pick up the baby when she falls over. He is a man of action, not words — so different from Arthur.

In the early Seventies, I'm fortunate to finally meet another man of action and few words. We meet at a church dance and he breaks through my hardened defences slowly with his candour, wit and respectful behaviour. A seaman in the merchant navy, Donald McNiff is a gentle Scottish giant who doesn't even hold my hand until the day he gets down on one knee to slip a ring on my finger. By this

---

26. Eurasian: a mixed-race child, usually from Caucasian and South East Asian parents.

point, he's met my whole family and is an instant hit with Ginny. He treats her as though she is his own daughter and wants us to be a family, even though he knows that we won't be able to have a child of our own. We leave for Hertfordshire a few years later in 1975 when Ginny is sixteen. My mum is heartbroken because she has helped to bring Ginny up as one of her own. She begins English language lessons so she can write to us. A year later, aged seventy-five, she finally masters the language, and the love she feels for us is evident in her carefully formed cursive script and well-worded phrases.

My Mum: Theresa
(Ang Pek Tho, DOB 31 March 1932)

"HIS NAME IS Peter McGrath, Lil. I call him Pete, but everyone else calls him Mac. He's in the Army, but is leaving to start a new job in London soon and wants me to go with him. Once we're both settled, we'll get married in London. I'll send for you and Ginny as soon as I've saved enough money. Ginny could be a flower girl at our wedding. It's going to be so dreamy and I can see her toddling up the church aisle, flowers in her hair, dressed in a summery yellow dress." I've been dating Pete since we met at the Catholic Centre six months ago, but I'm only now telling Lil because I'm mindful of how she might feel after Arthur. Pete has been stationed out in Singapore for a few years with the British Army but has found a civilian job in Security that offers more money and better prospects.

"Sa, that sounds wonderful. I'm so happy for you!" she hugs me tightly. "Er … I'm not sure how to say this, but I hope you're being careful and learning from my mistake. Remember not to sleep with him until that ring is firmly on your finger!"

"Of course not! All we've done is kiss. Of course he wants more, but I know both you and Mum will kill me if I give in! Can you imagine Mum's and Pa's faces if Ginny number two came along!" We dissolve into nervous laughter, falling back onto the bed, at the thought of our parents' shock and dismay.

My mum is surprisingly supportive of my move to London, even though I am the only one of her daughters who still wears the traditional Peranakan sarong kebaya. I guess having three unmarried daughters in their mid to late twenties is a worry for her. By age twenty-five, she'd been married for eight years and already had six children.

Just before I board the ship, she presses some pound notes into my hand. I try to return the money but she just holds me tight and whispers,

"It's the least I can do. You never got the chance to go to university because your pa and I ran out of money. I've always been so proud of how you taught yourself to become the best copy typist there is, graduating top of secretarial school. Now go be amazing!"

That was three months ago. I sigh as I carve off a small piece of chicken from the nearly bare carcass. Tomorrow, I will go to the food market near Praed

Street in Paddington to buy another chicken that I will roast in the small oven in my small bedsit, and it will last me all week. Pete and I rarely see each other because we're always working and he lives an hour away in a different part of London. This is not at all what I expected and I haven't been able to save much due to the high cost of living. How I yearn for Singaporean hawker stall food and my mother's homemade chicken curry with sambal belachan. I'm meeting Pete shortly though, so I stop feeling sorry for myself and slap some makeup on for my beloved.

It's so good to see him. He hugs me close and tells me I'm a sight for sore eyes. "You're not too shabby yourself!", I reply in return, especially as I notice how the other women in Hyde Park are checking out his dark, tousled hair and baby blue eyes. We spend most of the time catching up on what's happened since we last met up three weeks ago. Until he gets down on one knee and produces a small, plain silver ring.

"Theresa Ang, please make me the happiest man on the planet and marry me. I've applied for a marriage licence and I won't take no for an answer!"

He slips the ring on my finger and kisses me softly on the lips. We're drunk on love and spend the rest of the afternoon planning our future. We decide that financially, we'll be a lot better off living in one place rather than paying rent for separate properties. After scrapping together every last pound, shilling and penny for the last three months, it will be such a relief to have money left over to buy more than one chicken a week. I feel more positive than I've felt for ages, but a niggling worry at the back of my mind prompts me to ask Pete,

"What happens if I lose my job or can't work because we decide to start a family?"

He ponders my question for a long while, standing up and moving away from me, "Well, best you make sure you're never out of a job then!"

Suddenly, I'm aware of how cold it is now that the winter sun has set. I feel so shivery and bereft of hope that even the

Great Fire of London wouldn't be able to warm me up. We talk for a while longer, but my mind is preoccupied with worrying about our future.

A week later, I slip my plain silver band into an envelope and put it in the post to Pete. I book my passage to Singapore and work out my months' notice. Four roast chickens later, I'm back home where I belong.

It isn't long before I'm back in the swing of things and I find a job as a copy typist in the typist pool at the Hong Kong and Shanghai Banking Corporation in the City. It's an entry level job and our office is located in the basement of the skyscraper, the top floor being reserved for the CEO. I miss my handsome Pete, but I don't miss the smog in London or the skinny chickens. He's written every day for six months asking me to reconsider but I'm not prepared to marry a man who doesn't have a plan to provide for me and our future family. I celebrate my thirtieth birthday with some girlfriends, drinking coffee and eating chocolate cake, pretending we're in Paris. I'm happy, but every time I look at Ginny or hold her little hand to cross the street, my heart feels like it's missing something vital.

A year later, I'm rushing to cross the busy street on my way to work when my heel gets caught in a drain grate, sending me flying into the strong arms of a good-looking Chinese guy, who seems just as surprised as I am. He retrieves my shoe and slips it onto my foot as if I'm Cinderella and he's Prince Charming. We laugh off our mutual embarrassment, and as he's walking in the same direction, we start conversing along the way as if we're old friends. His name is Phillip and when we get to my office, he immediately asks for my phone number. I'm usually shy, but his cordiality and jovial manner puts me at ease, so I oblige. Phillip calls me that evening and asks me out on a date.

I finally realise what Mum and Lil mean when they describe

what it's like to fall in love. Everything and everyone seems to fade into the background, while the person you love becomes the sole focal point for your attention. Opposites attract, they really do. I'm introverted, he's extroverted; I'm a homebody, he's a party animal; I'm cautious while he rushes headlong into everything. Before I know it, we're engaged to be married and I let my guard down before the wedding date is set, when he promises me he'll look after me forever.

He's met my family who find him very charming and he's certainly passed the Pa test — I think Pa is secretly relieved that one of his daughters will end up with a Chinese man. All is going swimmingly until the morning I am violently sick. I'm convinced it's just stomach flu or gastroenteritis but it carries on for over two weeks. Lil has her suspicions, so she makes me go to the local sinsei who confirms that I am pregnant. I'm genuinely excited about the news and I am sure Phillip will be too. We'll just have to bring forward our wedding plans. I tell him that evening and fully expect him to be just as excited as I am. Instead, he falls silent and looks down at the floor. He starts to speak, so softly that I have to lean in to hear his shocking confession.

"I'm truly sorry Theresa, but I'm already married. I was going to tell you about it but I wanted to wait till after I got divorced and I was free to marry you. My wife and I got married when we were very young and impulsive. We don't love each other anymore but just never got around to getting a divorce."

I'm reeling with shock, but I think on my feet and suggest that he can tell her about us and the baby. Surely then she would agree to the divorce and we can get married before the baby arrives.

He shakes his head sadly and still doesn't look at me.

"What's the matter now? Please Phillip, just tell me!"

"Well, er ..." He stands up and shifts his weight uneasily from foot to foot, "um, the thing is, I went home drunk two months ago and we ended up sleeping together, so er ...well, um ..."

"For God's sake Phillip, just spit it out!" My anger is rapidly overtaking my dread.

Finally he looks me in the eye and sighs, "She's pregnant too."

#

I CRY ALL the way to the hospital until they put me under general anaesthetic. Lil wordlessly holds my hand and gives it the occasional squeeze. At least I found out early enough to take appropriate action, and I'm old enough so I don't need parental permission. Phillip has paid for a top gynaecologist to perform the Dilation & Curettage procedure. It's the least he can do, Lil scoffs angrily, after lying to you and proposing under false pretences. Her words just make me cry harder, so she stops speaking. I'm violently sick when they rouse me after the operation, sadly not due to the baby anymore, but because of the strong anaesthetic. I cry all the way home, mourning the loss of my baby, the demise of my relationship, and the obliteration of any trust I had left in men and love.

#

"YEE SI CHOR-LANG[27]!", my mum shakes her head disapprovingly after meeting Stephen. I admit that we're both from totally different walks of life; my pa, who sadly passed away a few months ago, would probably disapprove too because Stephen's family is working class; they socialise in different circles and don't speak the same dialect. I'm anxious to change her mind about him, but she points out that we've had a whirlwind romance, that he's ten years younger than me, and that six months is simply not enough time to work out if the man I've met is The One. I remind her that this isn't my first rodeo and that at thirty-three, my biological clock is ticking. Anyway I add, it's a good thing he's younger than me because that way, he'll be able to look after me when I'm old.

---

27. Yee si chor-lang: Hokkien phrase for 'He is a rough person, an uncouth man'.

We've both been unlucky in love and even though I've told him about Phillip, he still pursues me with passion, writing me a poem a day until I agree to marry him. We marry in November 1965 despite my mother's misgivings. I leave home to live in a small bedroom in a flat we share with his older half-brother and another couple. It's near the Naval base in Sembawang, where Stephen is an accountant. Before long, as the British pull out of Singapore, Stephen finds a new, better-paid job as a salesman and begins to drink heavily when he's out entertaining customers. He was badly abused as a child by his pa, who used to physically chastise his mum and him for just breathing. I suspect he was simply venting his frustrations on his second family because his first wife died in childbirth. One beating my mother-in-law endured was so severe that she lost the child she was carrying.

To make ends meet, Stephen holds down two jobs and we still have little to no money left every month after giving our respective parents their monthly allowance. After a month, my mum refuses to take her allowance but my father-in-law insists on it. We're poor but mostly happy. Six months into our marriage, Stephen asks if I can accompany him to a customer dinner. When we're there, he tries to ply me with alcohol but I refuse to drink. The minute we get home, fuelled by drunken rage and no doubt his childhood memories of domestic violence, he lashes out at me. The next morning, I try my best to cover up my black eye with make-up, while he apologises profusely and swears on his own life that he will never do it again. Having never experienced

any violence before, I'm reminded of my mum saying that he's chor-lang and dread to think what she will say now. I try not to rile him so I stop attending customer dinners and pretend to be asleep when he comes home very drunk.

One night, I sense he's in a different, more dangerous, mood. He wakes me up and tries to make love to me. I refuse his advances because he stinks of alcohol and we both have to be up at 5am. The beating is more severe this time round, so much so that make-up doesn't cover all the bruises. I have to wear dark glasses instead and pretend I have a migraine so other people won't wonder why I'm wearing them. Later that evening, my mum (who insists I join her for a family dinner) makes me take off the glasses. She weeps when she sees the state of my face. I stay with her for two weeks till the bruising is almost gone, during which time, Stephen tries to see me every evening, and when refused entry by my mum, stands outside calling out for me, crying and apologising.

I relent. I go back to him because I can't bear another failed relationship and the stigma of divorce. Besides, the Catholic faith does not permit divorce and I don't want my soul to burn in Hell forever. By the time Stephanie is born in January 1968, things seem to have settled down. I feel as if God has finally forgiven me for my sins because at thirty-five, I was beginning to think I would never be blessed with children as punishment for the abortion. Soon after, I fall pregnant again but the baby (a boy) is prematurely stillborn at 24 weeks. We're blessed with another daughter, Simone, in November 1969, who refuses to sleep and constantly cries unless she's being held. I fall ill from floor-walking every night to soothe her to sleep. Another boy is miscarried at 22 weeks just before my fortieth birthday and we stop trying for another. I tell Stephen that we have to do everything within our power to ensure our daughters do not follow in the footsteps of Lil and me. They deserve the bright futures that we were both denied.

My Maternal Aunt: Philomena
(Ang Pek Eng, DOB 22 February 1934)

MY SISTERS ARE so much more vivacious and far prettier than me, but I'm perfectly happy to have grown up in their shadow. I'm the worrier in our family, nervous about almost everything, always fussing over Ginny or looking out for Lucy, the adopted daughter of my pa's second wife who's actually younger than me! After the war, my pa planned to send her to work as a sing song girl in one of the Smith Street or Temple Street teahouses, but my mum decided to accept her into our family because we all knew the teahouses were just poorly disguised brothels.

Lucy is a worry for us all. Orphaned when her mother, a pei pa chai, died straight after her birth, no one knew who her father was. My pa's second wife adopted her out of pity. I am eight when I meet her in 1942, a pretty girl with a cheeky twinkle in her eyes. We're forced to live in the same house as my pa's second wife who refuses to live outside of the city; a few months later when the Japanese take over all the central districts, Lucy flees with us to the Kampong, entertaining us with her singing and dancing. At just three years old, she's very sure of herself and soon weaves her way into our hearts. I become Lucy's 'mum' which my family finds funny because there are only six years between us!

Living in the jungle scares me senseless. Even before the war began, my parents had to let most of our servants go because they had run out of money, so Lil, Sa and I are responsible for all the chores. It's my job to hang out the washing, fold it when it's dry and then bring it back in. Lucy tries to help but is too tiny to even reach the bamboo poles perched precariously in between the banana trees, let alone peg out the clothes and bedsheets. My mum constantly reminds us to bring the washing in as soon as it's dry to avoid it being deluged during the tropical thunderstorms. She also warns us never to leave the washing out overnight or it will become bloodstained when the Pontianak[28] fly past in the dead of the night. I forget on one occasion. After a restless night lying half-awake and listening to the strange, distant wails of what sounds like a crying baby, I go out to gather the white bedsheets. I'm horrified to find them stained red (apparently from Pontianak blood), but Lucy calmly tells us, in a very matter-of-fact way, that it was just her mummy coming to visit.

I spend most of my late teens working in the library and walking to and from school to pick Lucy up. One morning, I realise I've forgotten to hand over her lunchbox, so I walk back. I'm surprised to see her leave school furtively, so I follow her. Imagine my dismay when I see that she's gone into one of the Smith Street teahouses, no doubt curious about her birth mother. I tell Sa that evening, because she's better placed to discipline Lucy; I haven't got the stomach for it. That night, Sa scolds Lucy and canes her until her legs are covered in angry, red welts and she's a blubbering mess. I feel really bad and go to confession every day for a month to ask for forgiveness, even though I know that Sa is only being cruel to be kind.

I am so shy and retiring that it's a wonder really when I eventually meet and marry Eng Swee, a secondary school teacher who likes to read as much as I do; in fact, that's how we meet — in the library where I work. My mum is as surprised as I am because she's resigned to me remaining a spinster for the rest of my life. I'm the last of her children to marry and she can finally relax now I'm no longer her responsibility. We start trying for a baby immediately. Having helped to bring up Ginny and Lucy, I'm keen to become a mum before I'm thirty-five.

After three years, we're still unable to conceive. Eng Swee and I sit in the waiting room of the private hospital, nervously awaiting our appointment with the reproductive endocrinologist following a barrage of tests and scans.

"Come in, come in, Mr and Mrs Tan. I have your test results

---

28. Pontianak: A mythical vampiric ghost of a woman who has died in childbirth and whose bloody spirit form resides in banana trees.

here and am ready to explain what it all means. Mr Tan, we'll start with you first. No problems with hormone levels or sperm count, everything is normal, all good there! Right, now Mrs Tan, I'm afraid I have bad news. Your scan results indicate that you have a unicornuate uterus." She pauses when she sees how confused I am by her use of medical jargon.

"What it means is only half of your womb developed at birth so even if you do get pregnant, you're likely to miscarry the foetus before twelve weeks. Or worse still, you may have an ectopic pregnancy where the fertilised egg implants in your fallopian tube, which then ruptures as the foetus develops. What I'm trying to say is, you may be better off considering adoption if you would like to have a baby soon."

My head is reeling with too much information. Eng Swee pays the exorbitant bill and holds my hand as we wander outside despondently to find thick black clouds gathering. The downpour that follows washes away my tears and strengthens my resolve to give a home to an orphan like Lucy.

Six months later, on Christmas Day, we welcome Rosalind into our lives. We know very little about her birth parents, only that they are married but are too poor to bring her up themselves. Eng Swee, in particular, tries his very best to teach her basic maths and english before she's old enough to go to

kindergarten, keen to get her off to a flying start. He is a good husband and father, his only vice being a penchant for betting on the horses. We all live in the same house as my mum, Lil, Sa and Laurence, so the cousins get to play with each other. Ginny and Lucy, as the older ones, are in charge of the youngsters. We are one big happy family. Ros is particularly close to Steph and Mone, Sa's girls; the three of them always getting up to mischief. One time, Ros and Steph think it would be fun to put Mone in a laundry basket and roll her down the stairs; thankfully, I manage to stop the basket before it rolls all the way down.

When the girls start school, Eng Swee and I notice that Ros struggles to keep up with homework. As she develops into her teens, her terrifying mood swings and physically challenging behaviour start to become an issue when, for example, she chucks a glass of water over Mone's head for no apparent reason while we're eating lunch at Pizza Hut. Mone shrugs it off but I can see how puzzled she is. Calmly, she asks Ros who made her do it and waits patiently for the answer.

"I don't know." replies Ros after a while, "But I can hear them in my head."

That is when we discover the voices Ros has been listening to. After many more months of investigation and mounting medical bills, we discover to our dismay, that Ros is suffering from schizophrenia. The doctors tell us that she will never be able to go through life unmedicated, hold down a job or even have a normal lifestyle. We are devastated for her, but as her parents, we continue to care for our girl because we love her very much, exactly as she is. Even though she was not born into our family, she is as much a part of it as I am.

Chapter 3
Love in Real Life

Why my Parents should get Divorced

EVERY GIRL WAITS for her Prince Charming to ride in on his white charger and save her from *her wicked stepmother / an arranged marriage / a fate worse than death / her dysfunctional family / herself (*delete or amend as you wish*).

I'm no different. I watch my Mum and Pa as I grow up, and I feel for them because they're clearly not experiencing a fairy tale romance, or even a normal, run-of-the-mill relationship. It's clear to me that they were riding this emotionally-charged relationship rollercoaster for years before I was born. They disagree about almost everything, even something as simple as what to have for dinner; they constantly argue, bicker and fight, sometimes physically. They alternate between heated screaming matches and icy cold-shouldering, but whatever state they happen to be in at any particular moment, they stick together stoically, martyr-like in their highly viscous and volatile union.

I inadvertently become the catalyst for the first truly explosive interaction between them when I am seven. My Mama, parents, Steph and I are living together in a rented two-bedroom bungalow in Lorong Stangee because Mama had to sell off our

Marshall Road mansion to pay off her debts when her business failed. Mama has her own room out of respect, and we mirror the same sleeping arrangements from before, the four of us sandwiched in a single room. I'm going through my tomboy phase, sporting a short haircut and living in jeans twenty-four-seven, only wearing school skirts because I must. I love to play outside in the large monsoon drains, catching tadpoles, bringing them home and watching them transform into frogs in one of the aquariums housed within our covered outdoor kitchen. On one of my tadpole hunts, I notice that Pa is huddled in the public telephone box at the end of the street, so deep in conversation that he doesn't see me. When I go back indoors, I ask Mum if our house phone is broken.

"No Mone, I think it's working. Go call the speaking clock to check."

I do as I'm told and confirm it's working fine.

"Why do you ask?" Mum inquires as she prepares dinner with Mama, while I stick the new tadpoles in the tank to get acquainted with their friends. Steph is in the living room studying as usual.

"Oh nothing really. I was just wondering why Pa is making calls outside in the telephone box, that's all. Maybe it wasn't working earlier."

I hear a plate smash as she drops it, then help Mama clean up the mess because Mum has rushed outside in a real hurry. Thinking nothing of it, I help Mama dish up dinner for just us three, and put some food aside for my parents for later. We're all in our bedrooms when we hear the front door slamming open, then shut. The familiar sound of raised voices carries into our bedroom and I hear the name 'Doreen' and the words 'cheating bastard', except something is different this time — Mum's crying hysterically, sobbing so hard that she's struggling to catch her breath. Steph and I creep out of bed and peek out the door, bodies tensely coiled, ready to spring back in case either of them turn around.

"I can't believe it! After everything I've put up with, you're having an affair with some slut who's only interested in you because you buy her presents. You're spending our hard-earned money just to fuck her chow[29] zee-bai[30], rather than looking after your family like a real man! I'll cut off your lang-jiao[31] just to see if that will make you a better person! You make me sick! Go, get out! Get out and go stay with her in sin! You cheating bastard!"

With that, she charges into our room so quickly, we have no time to jump back into bed, so we just stand there like startled rabbits in the headlights. She hugs us close, chest heaving, trying to collect herself. Unsure how much we've heard, she tells us that Pa is going away on an emergency business trip, indefinitely. We watch wordlessly as she pulls out his suitcase and clothes, stuffing everything in hurriedly and carelessly, and flinch when she flings the heavy case at him. I notice then that he's crying too. He looks guilty and defeated.

"I'm sorry." Pa says, as he leaves.

I feel like it's my fault that Pa's gone. I shouldn't have said anything.

#

WE CARRY ON regardless. Mum still wakes up at 5am every morning, except Sunday, to cook our lunch before she leaves for work, and doesn't come home till 7pm. The tense and stressful pressure-cooker ambience has been replaced by wistfully sad and sober overtones now that Pa has been removed from the equation. Unfortunately, the ceasefire is short-lived. After a month of whispered, late-night conversations that Mum thinks we can't hear, Pa returns home with his tail between his legs. Apparently, she's given Pa an ultimatum — give up his mistress or give up his family. So, family it is!

By now, almost everything in our Lorong Stangee rental has been packed into boxes because we are moving into a condo

---

29. Chow: Hokkien word for smelly.

30. Zee-bai: Hokkien word for vagina, but ruder (cunt).

31. Lang-jiao: Hokkien word for penis.

at Laguna Park which overlooks the East Coast Park area, very close to the sea. Both Mum and Pa have been rewarded for their hard work — Mum's been promoted to become the personal assistant to the CEO of HSBC Singapore, and Pa is now sales manager at Stanley Tools. Financially, we're in a good place. The apartment has three bedrooms (one ensuite), separate kitchen, dining and living areas, a balcony and stunning views. Pa will sleep in the ensuite master bedroom on his own, Mum, Steph and I will share the middle bedroom and Mama will have the third bedroom. I choose to sleep on a pull-out bed so Mum and Steph can have more space to stretch out on the double bed. Our bedroom has amazing floor-to-ceiling built-in wardrobes with mirrored sliding doors, and a long fitted desk running along the wall with sliding windows and safety grilles.

Mama hasn't been working since her business failed; she is learning how to read and write English so she can correspond with Tua Ee and Ginny. Steph studies almost all of the time, so I'm either listening to Mama's stories about her extended family, or helping her with English language lessons. Mama tells me that she has a new nickname for Pa — she calls him Tao-Hong[32] because she thinks he's mentally unhinged. Mum has told her all about the abuse he suffered and witnessed as a child. She's also seen how much he drinks, and how it unleashes his anger and turns him into someone we don't recognise. I can tell that she's worried about Mum. To lighten the mood, I ask Mama to tell me a love story with a happy ending.

"One of my Pa's cousins was a very good man who worked very hard, seven days a week. He never complained and would get up every day to make breakfast for his wife and three children before going to work. He never drank, smoked opium or gambled and always provided for his family. But Mone, only the good die young because he died from cancer, like your kongkong, when he was in his fifties."

---

32. Tao-Hong: Hokkien word meaning crazy or mentally unstable, literally translated as 'head windy'

I am intrigued by the idea that good men actually exist, because this is so far removed from the stories Tua Ee and Mum have told me about the men they've encountered. Mama sighs before she bursts the rose-tinted bubble, "The thing is, when my cousin died, an unknown woman with two young children turned up at his wake. They were his second family. Seems that each wife thought he worked seven days a week because he would divide his time equally between them. So Mone, the moral of the story is — you can't say that a man is good until you've checked for the skeletons in his closet, and he's been buried for at least six months!"

"Mama!" I exclaim while laughing, "You were supposed to tell me about a love story with a happy ending!"

"But it was a happy ending. Ignorance is bliss. Both his families were happy right up until the end!"

We're both laughing loudly now, so loudly that Steph pointedly shuts Mama's room door with an irritable flourish before slamming our room door shut, the noise we're making clearly interrupting her revision. But that only makes us laugh even more.

THE NEXT EXPLOSIVE interaction takes place when I'm nine. Pa has an important black tie dinner to attend and he wants to impress his new French boss, so for once, Mum is going with him. She looks really glamorous in her floor-length shimmering gold-sequinned dress and high-heeled stilettos with matching clutch bag. I wish I could look like my mum when I grow up. Mama, Steph and I see them off as they wait for the lift, then we lock the front door, have dinner and get ready for bed.

A few hours later, I wake up suddenly, startled by the familiar sound of raised voices.

"Stephen, STOP IT! You're drunk, just go and sleep it off!", Mum sounds frightened.

"Why do you ALWAYS embarrass me, Three-sah? Why? You know I need to impress my new boss but you refused to drink. Why come if you're not going to drink and eat Western food because of the Goo-nee[33] smell? Then you spent all night talking to the Ang-mohs, letting them look down your dress at your breasts, making me look like an IDIOT, A stupid Chinese CUCKOLD! You want to be fucked by Ang-moh lang-jiao, go ahead! Don't let me stop you!"

"Stop it Stephen! Stop it! I work with Ang-mohs every day and I'm not the one who cheats. You are! With that slut Doreen!"

"Why do you always have to throw that in my face? Why do you always have to bring up the past? You've turned the girls against my family, you nag me when I see my mum, you don't even like me to meet up with my brothers and sister. What's wrong with you?"

"You know what's wrong with me? You're what's wrong with me! My mum is right — you are tao-hong! Crazy for crawling back to your bastard father after he gave you syphilis when you were born, crazy for kowtowing to him every time he demands something. Why don't you stand up to him? Where are your balls? And you call yourself a MAN!"

There's a sudden loud thud, followed by the sound of something smashing, followed by a worrying silence. I leap out of bed, shaking Steph awake, I can't believe she's slept through all the shouting and screaming. "They're fighting again, Steph. Wake up! I think it's serious this time!"

Right on cue, my parents burst into our bedroom and the blinding light flicks on. Mum's beautiful dress is ripped and torn; I can see her bra. Her shoulders and neck look sore and red as if she's been grabbed and shaken hard like a rag doll. She's holding her stilettos heel side up, one in each hand. She looks simultaneously scared and angry, makeup smudged and smeared all over her face like a Wayang[34] actress. She backs into the room towards us as Pa advances menacingly with balled, raised fists, like a boxer weighing up where he should land his next sucker

---

33. Goo-nee: Hokkien word for dairy, literally translated as 'cow breast'.

34. Wayang: Chinese opera

punch. He strikes out hard with his right fist, but misses as Mum ducks, so his fist smashes into the mirrored door of our wardrobe and the glass pieces scatter like broken dreams all around us. Some of them are embedded in his fist which starts to bleed. He's oblivious to this and goes in for another punch, this time with his left fist. Mum is too quick for him. There's more blood and shattered shards spraying everywhere. Mum strikes him on the head with the heel of her stiletto, drilling a hole which starts to bleed when she pulls back. Pa recoils in shock, momentarily stunned into inaction.

I hear someone screaming loudly "NOOOOOOOOOOOO!".

I realise it's me and see Mama at the door, looking horrified and upset. Mama unleashes a torrent of Hokkien abuse at Pa, trying to distract him as he picks up the iron Buddha ornament near our desk and advances towards Mum. Mum grabs both of us, swiftly pulling us towards the long desk. She slides the window wide open and pushes the safety grille to one side. She pulls herself, then us, up onto the desk and leans towards the unbarred, open window.

"I swear to God Stephen! If you take one more step towards us, I'll jump out of this window and take the girls with me. You can live with that on your conscience! Don't push me Stephen. I WILL DO IT!"

Mum's suicide threat hangs in the air like a nuclear bomb about to detonate. Steph and I are wailing so loudly that lights begin to switch on in neighbouring apartment blocks. Pa stops. I can see the red mist of rage lifting from his eyes. Now he's sobbing too and he begs Mum incoherently to come down from the desk as he retreats out of our room, bleeding from his head, hands and feet like a sinner on the cross.

Mama helps us down from the desk. Steph is still crying, but I've stopped now. I have no tears left to cry, and no words to describe the horror. I can hear Pa wailing in his room like an injured animal. So can Mum, who's holding and rocking Steph to calm her down. She tells me to go tend to his wounds, and gestures towards the first aid kit in the wardrobe. I walk robotically into Pa's bedroom, first aid kit in hand. He's so drunk, he barely recognises who I am. I can feel his pain as I clean up and bandage his wounds while he whimpers unintelligibly. But an angry voice pipes up in my head: *Who's the parent here, Pa? Who's looking after who?* The voice softens, becoming sad and forlorn: *You're supposed to look after me.*

A solitary tear slides down my left cheek. Aged nine, it feels like my childhood is over.

Mama helps Mum and me to clean up the mess while Steph sleeps. As the first rays of light peek over the horizon, Mum hugs me close and tells me she's going away for a while to teach Pa a lesson. She can't say where she's going because she doesn't want him to know. I nod, suddenly mute again. *Why can't you just take us with you*, my heart cries out. But I say nothing. She leaves a note for Steph and kisses her gently on her forehead. The front door clicks shut. "Please Mum, don't go!" I whisper, too late.

I'm determined to ensure that everything carries on regardless. Steph is back in her revision routine — I guess that's her way of escaping the misery. A pragmatic approach works better for me, so I help Mama cook, wash the dishes afterwards, clean the kitchen, sweep then mop the floors and hand wash the clothes just as Mum does.

After scrubbing the clothes on the washing board, I rinse them out in another pail, and wring them to squeeze out excess water. I peg the clothes on long bamboo poles, then manoeuvre them out of the window, holding onto one end so I can slot it into the pole holder that protrudes out of the external wall. I have to stand on a stool because I'm still small. I nearly fall out

of the window just as I'm hanging out the fourth and final pole. The combined weight of the pole with heavy wet clothes is too much for my centre of gravity; I lose my balance and start to slide forward. For a split second, I contemplate allowing myself to fall, but survival instinct kicks in, and I hook my right leg around the window frame, somehow managing to hold onto the pole as well. I find a way to do it in the end, but I suddenly feel angry, inexplicably angry, at Mum, for leaving me here to deal with everything.

#

TWO WEEKS LATER, Pa is going mad with guilt and worry because he still doesn't know where Mum is. He thinks she's left him for good. Mama told me she's been staying with one of her friends and took two weeks off work to get away from everything. I know she's coming home tonight just after dinner time. As soon as I finish washing and drying the dishes, I go to my pull-out bed and lie down with my eyes closed. Ten minutes later, Steph stops studying and tries to shake me awake so we can welcome Mum home. I keep my eyes shut and pretend to sleep. I hear them all greeting and hugging each other, Pa included, as if World War III didn't just happen two weeks ago. Finally, Mum creeps to the side of my bed and I hear her whisper, "Mone, are you awake? Mone, Mummy's home."

I refuse to respond, keeping my eyes stubbornly closed.

I think aloud angrily — *How long before you go away again?*

Then defiantly — *We were fine without you, we coped.*

Finally, tired now — *Just leave me alone. I'm still mad at you.*

I hear Mama tell her that I'm just tired from doing all the housework, and I'm glad that at least someone notices and cares.

All I Need is Love

I ALWAYS WANTED a dog. To experience the pure and unconditional feeling of being loved, just the way I am. To love another completely without wishing for anything more than mutual happiness. To always be enough.

Mum, obsessed with cleanliness, says, "We can't, because dogs are dirty. Besides, we are too busy to look after a dog and you have asthma!" Disappointed, but accepting that 'I want doesn't get', I spend most of my time outdoors cuddling and stroking other people's pet dogs, despite suffering from allergic rhinitis as a result. It's worth it, I think, just to feel the love in a wet-nosed lick and see the unquestioning devotion in their warm-brown eyes.

I learn about familial love at Mama's knee, when I see how she pores over English language books so she can write to Tua Ee and Ginny and read their replies. I observe how compassionate she is to everyone, even my pa, trying not to judge and always looking for the good in others. I experience love in Mum waking early every morning, without fail, to ensure we eat before we start our day. I feel Pa's love for us when he cooks our favourite food at weekends, spending hours prepping on his precious days off.

Over time, the books I read teach me that romantic love comes in many guises – brave, noble and pure like Jane's love for

Mr Rochester, which finally rewards him with the redemption he deserves; fateful and forbidden, like Romeo's love for Juliet leading to their untimely deaths; tragically exploitative and unforgiving until it's far too late, as poor Tess Durbeyfield discovers; tempestuously self-destructive for Cathy and her darkly vengeful Heathcliff; triumphant over pride, prejudice and societal norms for Darcy and Elizabeth; and timelessly enduring like Florentino's lifetime devotion to childhood sweetheart Fermina, their love finally blossoming in old age.

In real life, I only witness romantic love being toxically needy with Mum and Pa, who are always walking that tightrope of incompatibility, that thin line between love and hate.

When Mama passes away on Singapore's National Day in 1982 three months before my thirteenth birthday, I realise that love and loss are flipsides of the same coin. I sit by her open coffin for the entire three-day wake, reluctant to leave before we've finished the final silent conversation of our long goodbye. I tell her how much I will miss her wisdom, her humour, her selflessness, her anecdotes, her stories with not-so-happy endings, her generosity and kindness, her care and love. I will miss helping her with letters to and from the UK, I will miss defending her against Steph's scolding when she spills the Carnation condensed milk, I will miss her teaching me to knit ...I will just miss *her*. Mama is cremated along with gold paper ingots, pearls in her mouth, coins in her hands and across both eyes, ensuring she has everything she needs to be comfortable in the Afterlife. Despite the family converting to Catholicism decades ago, in death, Mama has returned to her Taoist roots.

Life resumes its normal, numbing rhythm soon after Mama's burial, sweeping us up and along in its busy-ness so I barely have time to grieve her loss. Mum and Pa work round the clock to achieve the Singaporean Dream, Steph studies, and I begin to develop a deep-seated longing for love. I long for someone to bare my soul to, someone who will accept my idiosyncrasies and imperfections, someone to be strong when I can't be, someone to love. I begin to feel an ache deep within me, a burning need to know how it feels to be touched in secret places, to be desired and wanted, to feel a fullness that completes me, an ache ever-present and constant. I dream in monochrome of a dark and handsome stranger, who though nameless, feels known to me. I can feel the fierce heat emanating from fumbling fingers across forbidden forests where no man has been before. I wake from these dreams with hot, flushed skin and lips that feel swollen and bruised, as if they've been ravished by passionate kisses from my dream lover.

NOT LONG AFTER my thirteenth birthday, I start my first bleed. Steph and I are waiting by the lift for Mum when our next-door neighbour, Mrs Lim, mum to two teenage boys, clears her throat awkwardly.

"Er Simone dear, you may want to go home and change your clothes before you go out." She gestures gently towards the back bottom-half of my purple polka dot dress. I twist my head round and look down, immediately dismayed and slightly perplexed to find a stain of red spreading slowly but surely for all to see. I grimace sheepishly, murmur my thanks, and rush back into our apartment with blazing cheeks of bright-red to match the stain. Mum is just on her way out of the open door as I slouch past her. She stops me and pulls me back by my arm, exclaiming loudly with Mrs Lim still within earshot, "Mone's lahsum lai liao[35]. Quick, get me some paper and a pen!"

I want to die. I cringe in excruciating embarrassment and disbelief as my mum pulls me into the dining area and commands me to stand still with my legs ajar, hurriedly pressing little balls of scrunched-up paper into my hand and instructing me to throw them between my legs. I do as I'm told, wishing the floor would open up and swallow me whole. Mum picks up the six balls of

---

35. Lahsum lai liao: Hokkien phrase literally translated as 'Dirty come already', an expression meaning that a woman's period has started.

paper furthest away from me and opens them up to reveal the numbers she will choose for the TOTO draw taking place later that evening. She starts filling them out on the betting slip while I stand forgotten, legs still spread wide, completely mortified and also confused about what's happening to my body. Surely I'm dying, so why is Mum obsessing over the lottery?

Eventually, Mum remembers that I'm still standing here. She grabs a box of sanitary towels out of the bathroom cabinet, chucks them at me and tells me to hurry and go change, so we can go out soon. She needs to get to the Singapore Pools store before the draw deadline. She's confident that she will win tonight because I always bring her luck, my birthdate having won her $5,000 in the 4D lottery when I was born. I change quickly. When we're on our way in the car, Mum explains that from now on, my lahsum will come monthly, during which time I will not be able to swim because tampons could rupture the hymen. She tells me that in some parts of China, a white cloth would be placed under a bride on her wedding night, and if the cloth is not stained red with the proof of her virginity the following morning the bride would be sent back to her family in shame, or publicly ridiculed for not being pure. It isn't until one year later, during a biology lesson, that I finally understand on an intellectual level the significance of menstruation. It's all very academic though, just a bodily function and a boring biological process in a textbook, nothing for me to personally worry about. Thirteen-year-old me is so gullible and innocent, yet to find out just how significant this day will be.

MAMA FIRMLY BELIEVED in fate and all things pre-ordained. I think so too, because so far in my life, everything seems to have happened for a reason. If Mama hadn't passed away, I wouldn't feel so alone and would have someone to confide in, someone who would listen without judging, someone to give me sound advice about bodies, boys and babies, having birthed twelve children herself in as many years. Instead, I carry on blithely reading romance novels, dreaming about Prince Charming saving me from my dysfunctional family and spiriting me away to begin our happily-ever-after.

Just after the end of secondary school semester one in June 1983, Steph and our friends, feeling footloose and fancy-free, hear about a party being organised by CHIJ[36] girls and SJI[37] boys.

It's Singapore's worst kept secret amongst us teenagers and the coolest party of the entire year with zero supervision, but our parents think it's a Church-organised event supervised by nuns and Jesuit priests because it's held on CHIJ premises. Mum gives her permission for us to attend as a reward for delivering top results again, and an incentive to do the same in the second semester.

The balmy evening air is buzzing with the sound of excitable girls dressed to the nines in sexy skirts short enough to be belts, low-cut tops showing off their Wonderbra-enhanced cleavages, and strappy sandals with heels so high I'm amazed their wearers can walk. Steph and her friends have gone for a more demure

---

36. CHIJ: Convent of the Holy Infant Jesus, girls-only Catholic convent school.
37. SJI: St Joseph's Institution, boys-only Catholic school run by Jesuit priests.

look in dark dresses with platform heels. It hasn't been long since my tadpole-collecting tomboy days, so I am acutely aware of how kahku[38] I look in a borrowed knee-length red skirt with a small slit at the back to allow movement, a loose-fitting, boat-necked white top with black artistic squiggles and black ballet flats. The only daring part of my ensemble is the V-shaped low back, which means I'm not wearing a bra. I'm very sporty, regularly running and swimming, so I don't really feel the need to wear one. As the youngest in our group of friends, I stick out like a sore thumb and eventually end up on the side lines while the others dance the night away with mostly older and very confident guys. SJI boys have a reputation of being pai-keah[39] which immediately makes them as desirable as forbidden fruit in the Garden of Eden. All the girls at the party are dying to dance with them. Everyone except me. They all just seem a bit immature.

I look down at my watch, bored already, the only saving grace about this party being the music. I close my eyes and feel my body swaying slightly to the beat, suddenly aware of the sultry scent of teenage pheromones surrounding me.

I sense him before I see him. Eyes still closed, I'm listening to Spandau Ballet as they begin crooning 'True', when I feel the heat of his stare and hear a deep voice whisper seductively in my ear. A fiery warmth mingling with his musky aftershave radiates over me hypnotically, setting my skin alight. I look up at a pair of deep-black eyes staring straight into my soul; he can't be more than three or four years older than me, but his dark swarthy skin tells me he comes from a mixed race heritage and piques my curiosity.

"Care to dance?" He doesn't wait for my reply but leads me onto the dance floor, pulling me really close so I fit snugly against his body in a strangely familiar way. He sings along with Tony Hadley, "this is the sound of my soul, this is the sound ..." I say nothing because no words are needed. A small gasp escapes my

---

38. Kahku: Singlish for Awkward/Clumsy.

39. Pai-keah: Hokkien for 'bad boy(s)'.

slightly parted lips when I feel his fingers brush my bare back ever so slightly, while his other hand pulls me even closer until my back arches, my breast pressed against his chest so our hearts meet, as he looks down, deep into my soul. I feel like I'm in my monochrome dream with my nameless stranger, everything around us fading away into non-existence.

When the song is over, we remain locked in close embrace even though the tempo of the next track is upbeat and faster. He pulls away reluctantly halfway through and whispers "Save the last dance for me" before walking away, while I somehow make it over on Bambi-like legs to Steph and our friends, who are staring open-mouthed in my direction.

"Oh my God, Simone! Do you know who that was?" asks Rachel.

I shake my head, suddenly mute again.

"He's the main DJ here tonight and word has it, he's very pai-keah! Didn't you feel all the daggers from the CHIJ girls when you were dancing? I can't believe it! Your first party and you bag the coolest guy of all! Wahlao[40], what's your secret?! You're not even wearing any makeup!"

I look over to where the DJ equipment is set up and recognise his tanned and toned body dressed casually in a black Calvin Klein T-shirt and dark blue jeans. He's put on a black hat since he held me on the dancefloor and is laughing in response to something the other DJ is saying. As if sensing my stare, he looks up and I feel my skin flush as he holds my eyes captive. Eons later, I look away, unable to shake that feeling of familiarity, blushing at the blatant desire I see in those dark eyes.

The hours fly by hazily while I sit around in a bit of a daze. The others have already forgotten what happened and are enjoying themselves elsewhere. I don't join them and turn down a few guys asking for a dance because I feel too distracted. I hear his voice announcing the last song for the night and look up just

---

40. Wahlao: Singlish exclamation meaning 'wow, OMG, good heavens, oh dear' to express surprise or disbelief.

as he holds out his hand to lead me onto the dance floor for the final slow dance of the evening.

"Hello again, I'm Adam."

"Hello Adam. I'm Simone."

"I know," he says as he envelopes me in an embrace that feels like home.

ADAM CALLS ME the next morning after we get home from Sunday mass. There's nothing casual about our conversation; he cuts straight to the chase. "I can't wait to see you again! Where do you live and I'll swing by?" His urgency ignites a primal response deep down inside me, the burning need from my dreams now a raging inferno. My imagination runs wild and I can feel myself blushing from top to toe like a shy schoolgirl who's been caught doing something very naughty.

"Er, well, we're on the East Coast in a condo estate called Laguna Park. But it's Sunday, my parents are home and I have school all week, so maybe next weekend?" I offer tentatively.

"Let's not leave it so long. Can you sneak out for a little while today? I really need to see you again. Please?"

My mind's already racing ahead to when I tell Mum and Pa about being needed at the tennis courts that afternoon. They probably won't even notice because Pa works most Sunday afternoons and Mum's always

watching some Chinese melodrama or TV series where couples fall in and out of love more often than I change my underwear.

"Okay, can you make it here for two? I'll meet you by the tennis courts" I whisper, throwing caution to the winds as I give him the address.

Adam holds out his hand as soon as he sees me and it feels like the most natural thing in the world to slip my hand into his, my fingers tingling from his touch. We walk through the underpass under the ECP to get to the beach and I ask him to tell me about himself. I listen intently as he says that he's basically my opposite — not particularly academic, no concrete plans for the future and a bit of a troublemaker at school. The only thing we have in common is our love of music and the magnetic attraction between us — a compelling need to be close, come what may. Logic tells me that this can't possibly work, but my heart urges me to give him a chance. We spend a few blissful hours chatting as if we've known each other for years, listening to the soundtrack of waves sliding onto, then away from the shore. He tells me I have the tiniest hands, while stroking my fingers so sensuously, I can feel his touch in the deepest and darkest corners of my soul. The sun is setting by the time we head back reluctantly. Turns out he's free all week and we agree to meet each day after I get back from school. Before he goes, he hugs me so close I can feel his heart beating faster and faster as his hands caress my body through my thin T-shirt, mirroring my own pulse, which is now racing rapidly. I respond by linking my hands around his muscular back and resting my head on his strong shoulder. We stay entwined for the longest time, just breathing each other in.

We meet almost every day and talk on the telephone when we don't. We tell each other everything — how disappointed he feels about his parents' strained relationship, his mum sleeping in one bedroom with his sister, him in another and his dad out in the living room on his own, their physical separation belying their deep emotional rift; I tell him how my parents have continued fighting, albeit less violently, with Mum and Pa appealing for Steph and me to take sides now that we're older. He shares his hopes to become an interior designer one day, and he encourages me when I confess I would prefer to do something artistic and literary rather than pursue the Singaporean Dream.

The first time we kiss by the sea, he tells me he loves me, cupping my face tenderly in his hands before gently brushing his lips across mine. Neither of us has kissed another before but instinct takes over, and within minutes, he's claiming my lips with more urgency, parting them with his tongue to explore the taste of my mouth. I respond with equal passion, that feeling of familiarity now intensifying into a feeling of fatedness. Even though we're from very different worlds, I say yes when he asks me to 'go steady' with him and to be his girlfriend.

NOT LONG AFTER my fifteenth birthday, Mum and Pa buy a condo at Dynasty Gardens on prestigious Sixth Avenue in Bukit Timah. Adam has enlisted for National Service but isn't due to start active duty for at least another year. I've met his family but we never spend much time at his home, because I have to focus on revising for my GCE 'O' Level[41] exams in my final year at St Nicholas Girls' School. Adam is a man of few words and prefers to express his feelings in a more physical way. Over the last few months, our dates invariably end up with both of us in his bed kissing and touching, always wanting to do much more, but stopping short, full of pent-up passion. Our relationship is still a well-kept secret from my parents, only Steph and a few of our friends know. I haven't dared to tell Mum because she's always warned us to stay away from men, to focus on studying hard and

---

41. GCE 'O' Level: General Certificate of Education (GCE) Ordinary Level, awarded as the secondary school-leaving qualification on a per subject basis.

getting into a UK university. In any case, with the relationship becoming increasingly passionate, the Catholic convent schoolgirl in me feels overwhelmed by crushing guilt that I am sinning by being unchaste. After years of attending catechism classes after Sunday mass, I've had it drilled into me that anything more than a peck on the cheek is sinning.

Adam begins to gate-crash parties organised by my local Parish Church just to spend as much time with me as possible before NS. One evening, while waiting for him to turn up, I end up talking to Andrew (a church friend about the same age as Adam); he tells me about some family issues he's experiencing. We're standing close to each other because of the loud music and he's having to bend his head and shoulders down towards me, so that I can hear him above the noise. All of a sudden, Andrew falls backwards away from me as he's pushed back aggressively by a very angry-looking Adam,

"GET AWAY FROM HER! How dare you touch my girlfriend!" His chest is heaving, fists clenched and ready to fight. I leap in between them while some mutual friends hold Adam back.

"It's not what it looks like Adam! Please stop. I love you, and only you. We were just talking." I'm crying, reminded of how Pa looked just before he smashed the mirrors in our room. By now, Andrew is on his feet and he backs off while Adam advances, "I saw the way you were looking at her. If I catch you doing that again, I'll kill you!"

Apologising profusely to Andrew, I try my best to calm Adam down and pull him outside into the garden, genuinely concerned because I have never seen him so agitated. His breathing is ragged and laboured and his eyes are wild as if possessed by a demon. It takes a good half-hour before he finally looks at me, tears in his eyes, "I can't lose you Simone. You're the only good thing in my life. I need you and you're no one else's but mine! Promise me you'll never leave me."

I hold him close, kissing away his tears, gently stroking his furrowed brow and anguished face, "I promise I'll never leave,

Adam. I promise I'm yours forever."

#

JUST BEFORE MY sixteenth birthday, Steph (now seventeen) meets Danny, the son of a rich Indonesian business man. Steph knows that Mum and Pa will approve because Danny comes from a wealthy and respectable family, so she tells them. My parents accept the relationship, giving me hope that they will do the same for me. They allow me to invite a few friends round for my sixteenth birthday party. I invite Adam, hoping that over time, I can introduce him as my boyfriend. Sadly, Mum takes an instant dislike to him, after he tells her where he lives and she learns about his humble background and poor academic performance. She doesn't even try to hide it. Pa is non-committal, perhaps more sympathetic, as he too came from a humble chor-lang background.

To avoid any aggro[42], we agree to keep our relationship secret for as long as it takes to win them round. After the party on our way downstairs, Adam gives me a simple gold ring for my sixteenth before he goes home. He holds me close and asks me to marry him, hopefully in a few years' time, when he's able to provide for me and any children we may have. I nod through happy tears and allow him to slip the gold band onto my ring finger, only taking it off (so my parents don't see) just before I walk back into the apartment.

Now that he's been to our estate and is known to the security guards, Adam starts coming around to mine while my parents are at work. We swim together, the cold water doing little to dampen our growing passion and desires, especially when we're both wearing skin-tight, skimpy swimwear. Ever since the church party, Adam's been very insecure and with every kiss, I feel his desperate desire to make me his, to possess me completely in every way, body, mind and soul. The shared swimming pool and

---
42. Aggro: Singlish for Aggravation.

sauna is hardly used by other residents during the week when they're at work, so we enjoy a fair amount of privacy.

On a wet Wednesday at the end of November a few weeks after he proposed, it's just the two of us swimming when the drizzle turns into a deluge. We rush into the sauna to take refuge and Adam locks the door from the inside to ensure we're not interrupted. His eyes are deep, dark pools of desire. In a heartbeat, he's pulled me into his arms, the hot steam rising off our glistening bodies as he tells me how beautiful I am, stealing my breath away with one ferociously hungry kiss after another, his tongue insistently demanding my surrender and submission. His hands are everywhere at once, at the base of my skull pulling my mouth closer into his, then squeezing, touching and caressing each and every inch of me until every single nerve in my body is crying out to feel him. A guttural, pleading moan builds from deep within me and escapes my lips when he moves to kiss my neck and lower, all sense and restraint gone. We are both undone by it, no longer standing, having collapsed onto the slick wooden slats of the sauna floor, skin-to-skin, trembling with emotion. I feel his hands pushing aside fabric in his urgent need for me and I can't, don't want to, stop him from making me his despite the stabbing pain. He's calling out my name and we're both riding the waves of pain-filled pleasure until I ask him to stop because we shouldn't be sinning like this. He tears himself away from me, breath ragged, body shaking, the only contact between us now his hand on my face, as he repeatedly says "I love you so much, I'm sorry Simone, but I just need you so much…"

Neither of us can breathe so we just sit there, holding each other, for the longest time.

We're not sure whether we actually did it. Steph is still at aerobics club, so we're sitting alone in my bedroom on my bed. I feel racked with guilt at how we allowed passion to get the better of us. I'm sure that all the Hail Marys in the world can't absolve us from this and we're going straight to hell on a one way ticket. Adam holds my hand, spinning the ring around my finger, and even though he doesn't speak a word, I can tell he's only sorry we stopped. He looks so sad.

"Penny for your thoughts?" I lean into him, resting my head on his chest, his arms circling me protectively as he replies,

"You know I love you, right?" I nod as he carries on. "I want to be a better person for you, prove your mum wrong, marry you and make love to you without having to sneak around. We don't need a piece of paper to tell us how we feel about each other. I'll never hurt you or leave you. Look at me, I want to see what's going on in those beautiful eyes." He tilts my face up towards his so he can see, then kisses me gently, trailing kisses up my neck, pausing to nip me playfully under my ear, and tracing my jawline with his wicked tongue until he reaches my lips.

We kiss longingly and I can feel his passion building again. The familiar ache returns with a vengeance, making it really hard for me to resolve the conflict I feel within. The Good Girl inside is warning me in loud, shrill tones, 'Stop kissing him! Go get dressed in the bathroom now Simone, before you do something you'll regret!' Whereas the She-Devil purrs temptingly in low, seductive tones, 'It's too late dear, you know it already happened earlier. If you really love him, you should make him happy. Show him how much you love him. After all, it's only a piece of paper! You've been together three years now, you're engaged, what are you waiting for?'

We fall back on my bed and I can tell Adam is now past the point of no return because his kisses are feverishly hot. He's pushing down the straps of my swimming costume with one hand and removing his trunks with the other. He pauses briefly just before taking off my costume completely, "Please be mine, please say yes, please make me the happiest guy in the whole world …" I lift my legs to make it easier for him to undress me, crying out a single yes under my breath but loud enough for him to hear. The pain that follows eclipses what I felt before. Adam feels my body tense up and stays very still, but I can see how much effort it's taking for him to resist the urge to move, so I close my eyes, push past the pain and give myself to him, allowing his body to possess mine completely. We're lost in the moment, overcome with emotion — love, guilt, pleasure and pain all merging into a swirling dark vortex of painful sensation, dragging us both down, deep down into damnation.

Afterwards, lying in each other's arms, the blood on the bedsheets telling us too late that we could have stopped after the sauna, and everything would still be all right, I ask myself a single question, 'How can something that feels so right be so wrong?'

We continue our clandestine meetings over the next few months, although we're not always able to do more than kiss, especially as his mum is a stay-at-home housewife and Steph is now at home a lot, revising for her exams. I'm secretly relieved, because I'm still guilt-ridden about what happened. Now that we've made love, Adam's possessiveness reaches alarming levels and he demands to see me more often, jealously monopolising my time and attention when we're on group outings, always asking about my activities at Hwa Chong Junior College and grilling me over every detail if I innocently mention any boys' names. A part of me understands why he behaves this way and tries to be patient, but another part of me feels frustrated at having to constantly explain myself, especially when I've already given him my *all*. We begin to argue when Frustration gets the better of Patience.

Before he starts his NS, Adam spends time with his cousin Colin and other old SJI friends when he's not with me. One weekday afternoon, while I'm working my way through a mountain of homework with essays coming out of my ears, Adam calls me out of the blue. I'm grateful for the distraction and happy to hear his voice. Within a minute though, I can hear his unhappiness and sense that he's trying to say something. I can even hear Colin in the background egging him on, "Go on, just do it! Stop being such a pussy!" He's in a public place surrounded by people and I can hear girls giggling nearby.

My heart fills with dreadful premonition before he even says it, "I think we should break up."

"What! Why? What have I done?" Tears are silently rolling down my cheeks.

"Nothing. I just wanna break up." His cold casualness cuts straight through me.

"Adam, please talk to me. We can't just break up without talking things through. Please help me understand what I can do to fix things. I know we've been arguing a lot recently, but surely you must know how much I love you. After everything we've been through together, you can't just throw it all away without giving me a reason. Please Adam. Just come round now and we can talk about it."

I can feel him wanting to say more before he sighs heavily, "There's nothing to talk about, I just don't love you anymore." The public telephone he's calling me from starts to beep, demanding more coins.

"Adam, please don't say that. I still love you, tell me what you want me to do …" The line goes dead as my now-frozen heart shatters into a million tiny pieces, each shard piercing deep into my soul. I sob, heartbroken and forlorn. "You didn't even say goodbye!"

I'VE LOST COUNT of the seconds, minutes, hours, days and months since Adam left me. After a long period of radio silence, I post the ring back to his home address, not even sure if he'll get it because surely, he must have already started his National Service. Steph is sympathetic but I don't trouble her with how I feel because I know she needs to focus on her revision. My closest friends at HCJC, Mave, Mun and Hock Seng, can see how sad I am and rally around trying to cheer me up. I don't divulge any details and try to move on with a smile on my face, not wanting to drag anyone else down. I spend hours late at night crying myself to sleep, wondering what I did wrong, coming up with a multitude of reasons why Adam decided to break up with me. I'm not pretty enough. Not desirable enough. Not generous enough. Not sexy enough. Not good enough. Not lovable enough. I can't decide whether it's one reason, a combination of reasons, or all of them. In the end, I'm left with a single overarching reason — put simply, it's just me. *I* am not enough. He just doesn't love me anymore.

WORD SOON GETS out that I'm 'available' through the Kaypoh[43] gossip machine. HCJC is the first co-ed college I've attended and I'm not familiar with the dating game, having been loyal to Adam since I was thirteen. Encouraged by my friends, I agree to go on a few first dates, but regret it within minutes of getting there because it all feels like child's play compared to my relationship with him. It's not their fault, it's mine; I'm just not emotionally available. I still long for him, even though he really hurt me, and I wonder how he is, whether he's happy. One of these first-date guys perseveres though, and Mave says I should just have a good time with him. Sam is boyishly good-looking, taller than Adam, with broad shoulders, and he makes me laugh. But when he kisses me, I don't feel the urge for more. My mum likes him though, and he often comes round to our place to study with me.

We're standing at the bus stop outside HCJC waiting to catch the bus home to Sixth Avenue when I feel goosebumps all over my body, the fine hairs at the base of my skull standing to attention like antennae sensing danger. Sam is laughing as he recounts a funny joke he heard this morning, when I suddenly

---

43. Kaypoh: Singlish for busybody.

sense Adam's stare and his brooding presence, just like our first dance when I sensed him before I saw him. I think I'm going crazy until I hear his voice "Hello Simone" — those two innocuous words unleash a torrent of mixed emotions within me, all jostling for the chance to utter the first word. I turn around to see his familiar face, thinner and more gaunt, hair cut very short, in military uniform, looking at me with dark desire, drinking in my soul as if I am still his, touching me all over, everywhere, with his oh-so-hungry eyes. Words fail me.

After what feels like years, Sam awkwardly excuses himself. I've not told him much about Adam, but he can tell by the way we're looking at each other that we need to be left alone. I can feel Adam bristling when Sam pecks me on the cheek to say goodbye and tells me he'll call me later. As soon as Sam leaves, Adam grabs my arm, pulling me closer to him, as he growls out his questions,

"Who is he? Why was he kissing you? How come he has your phone number?"

I instinctively start to explain until I realise, quite angrily, that he doesn't deserve any answers. I stay silent.

"Why aren't you saying anything? Say something Simone!" He shakes my arm vigorously as if that will make me spill all my secrets.

The bus arrives and I try to shrug off his hand to no avail. I've forgotten how strong he is. The first flames of wicked desire are starting to spark until, outraged at my body's wanton betrayal, I quash them down. "Let me go Adam. Please. I have nothing to say to you."

That's a lie, and we both know it. He corrals me in his arms in one swift movement, my palms trapped between our bodies, spread against his broad chest in a vain attempt to push him away. His mouth presses against mine in an instant, his tongue probing forcefully until I part my lips, my traitorous body taking over and responding with its own fierce, feral need of him, all those months of missing, yearning and longing poured into this one kiss.

"You. Belong. To. Me." he growls as he punctuates each word with one punishing kiss after another. When we eventually surface, he persuades me to walk with him to Coronation Shopping Plaza because apparently, we need to talk. A few months too late, I think, as we make our way there.

I'M CALMER NOW that the Beast Inside has been sated by the kiss that Sensible Me disapproves of. I have so many questions to ask, questions deserving of answers, but Adam is still upset about Sam, and I can see we won't get anywhere until I allay his fears. I am sparing with my answers though, giving enough detail to satisfy without stimulating further questions. I tell Adam the following: Sam is just a friend. He wants to be more than friends but we've only kissed. Nothing else. All of my friends have my number.

"So how many times has he kissed you? I bet an Ah Beng[44] like him doesn't know how to *really* kiss. He should stick with Ah Lians[45] because you're way out of his league!" he scoffs, disparaging poor Sam rather unfairly! But I smile gleefully on the inside because he still rates and ranks me highly. My Fairy Godmother has been busy waving her magic wand! I don't tell him that Sam is ex-SJI and is most definitely, not an Ah Beng.

"Now it's my turn. What happened that day when you called me to break up? What have you been doing since?"

He replies, clearly having given this a lot of thought, "You

---

44. Ah Beng: Singlish word for a male Chinese native who isn't westernised or cool.

45. Ah Lian: Singlish word for a female Chinese native who isn't westernised or cool.

were so busy with your studies, and we were arguing so much. I thought you didn't love me anymore because we weren't making love. So it seemed like a good idea to break up with you, before you broke up with me. Then, Colin and the guys were saying how I never go out with them anymore, and how unhealthy it is to be so obsessed about one girl. Especially a girl whose parents think I'm not good enough for her. When I told them I want to marry you, they said we're way too young and you'll just find someone else, someone better than me, when you go to the UK." He pauses, overcome with emotion, angrily wiping tears away on his sleeve. He's holding onto my hands so tightly that my knuckles feel bruised and stretched.

"I've been thinking of how I can make it up to you and persuade you to get back together with me. As soon as I said it, I wanted to take the words back, but it was too late. Then I had to go to camp the following week and I only get fourteen days of leave for the whole year. We can't take leave straightaway either. I tried to call a few times when I could, but you didn't answer because I guess you were at school. Or maybe you were kissing Sam! Did you do more than just kiss?" He looks like he really means what he's saying, so I keep listening, choosing to ignore his pointed remark and question.

"I got home this morning to dump my stuff before coming here to explain, and I found your ring. You said in the note that came with it, 'I still love you Adam, always will'. Did you mean it? I need to know if there's still a chance for us because I can't love anyone else the way I love you. I'm just no good without you, Simone."

This is so much to take in all at once. I have one last question that I need to ask, but I'm dreading the answer. "You just said you can't love anyone else the way you love me, Adam. Have you tried? I heard some girls giggling in the background when you called me to break up. Did you get together with one of them?"

I look him straight in the eye as I ask the question, the Chinese proverb 眼睛是心灵的窗户 (yǎn jīng shì xīn líng de chuāng hù)[46] comes to mind, because the eyes truly are windows to one's soul.

"Well, they hung out with all of us that day. Colin and I then went on a double date with a couple of them at the weekend but nothing happened. All I could think of, all I ever think of, is you!"

A sharp, stabbing pain paralyses my heart. I want more than anything to believe him, but what I see in my mind's eye is images of Pa huddled in the phone box on Lorong Stangee, whispering sweet nothings to his mistress, and Mum sobbing her heart out every night for a month after, their relationship irrevocably broken and damaged to this day. I see Adam kissing a perfect and beautiful girl, a girl who is enough; I see him touching her the way he touches me, and I am consumed by jealousy, that feeling of never-being-enough.

Adam holds my eyes with his steady gaze. "I'm willing to prove myself. I'll wait forever if you tell me that I haven't blown it, that there's still a chance I can make you mine again one day."

"I don't know Adam. I can't give you an answer right now. I just don't know if I can trust you again. Please give me time to think. I promise to let you know before your birthday."

"Okay," he agrees, holding my hands up to his lips and gently kissing each finger. "I'll wait. For as long as it takes."

#

WE TALK WHEN we can and he takes a day off to celebrate my birthday in early November. We go back to the beach at East Coast Park for a few hours and everything between us feels just like it did three and a half years ago. I stop seeing Sam soon after Adam comes back to me, although I don't tell him in case it gives him false hope. I think it would be unfair to continue when Sam and I have such different expectations and he wants much more than I am willing or able to give. Although I enjoy being single because, as Mum says, you don't have to watch the

---

46. 眼睛是心灵的窗户 translation: the eyes are the windows to the soul.

colour of someone else's face, I genuinely love Adam and want to be with him.

It's Christmas 1986, and we're at a church party when the DJ plays 'Last Christmas'. As we slow-dance to one of our all-time favourite songs, I remember our first dance to 'True'. Right on cue, Adam's hands feather my back in that same familiar way, and I still feel the same shivers down my spine now as I did then. I promised Adam I would let him know my decision before his birthday, so when the song ends, I tell him that I've decided to give 'us' another go. As long as he understands that I'll have to focus all my efforts on revising for my exams over the next year, because my parents are relying on me to do well and I can't let them down.

He's over the moon as he slips the ring back on my finger. He jokingly says it's been weighing him down for the whole time he's been carrying it around in his back pocket, waiting for me to say yes. We both agree to take things slow, and also to abstain from making love because of the guilt I feel. I know he's only acquiescing because it's what I want, which makes me love him even more.

On Adam's birthday, I surprise him with tickets to the 1986 re-release of 'Lady and the Tramp', not because we're into Disney movies, but because the back row of the dark and deserted movie theatre on New Year's Eve offers pitch-black privacy for his real birthday present. I don't think either of us remembers the movie, but we certainly welcomed 1987 with a big bang! I guess old habits die hard when all you want to do is make the one you love happy.

Adam returns to camp on 2nd January. Because of planned Army exercises, I don't see him again till early March, so we celebrate Valentine's Day belatedly. He invites me to his flat for an early dinner so I can get home before my parents. He's really pulled out the stops, setting up a romantic table for two in his bedroom, with me sitting on the edge of his bed, while he sits on his desk chair. He's serving a three-course candlelit dinner that he's cooked from scratch, complete with Snowball cocktails. His mum and sister are in the bedroom next to us but he locks his door for privacy.

We are halfway through the main course when, drunk on cocktails and love, I lean over to give him a kiss of appreciation. We share a tender, sweet kiss full of love and longing, but I sense the electric undercurrent of desire lying latent, buried beneath the surface of the promises we made last Christmas. Promises of abstinence, taking things slow and giving me the time I need to focus on what's important to me.

He looks at me, eyes darkly passionate with need, wordlessly pleading with me to reconsider. His eyes beg me to choose love over logic, passion over prudence, him over me. I *know* I shouldn't, the logical dreamer in me torn between doing what makes most sense, and what feels like following my dreams of finding love and happiness. After everything we've been through, I feel an almost primal need and obligation to give in to our desires because it will make him happy.

In the end, I make my choice by listening to my heart, not my head. And that is why, aged seventeen, I face the impossibly difficult decision of whether to end our unborn baby's life.

Interlude 1

As you join me on my journey, please take a musical break and listen to the song that captures the mood of that particular moment in time. Or read on.

The choice is yours.

'Hard to Say I'm Sorry', *song from the album 'Chicago 16' by Chicago, released July 1982*

Part Two
Me, Singapore & UK
(1988 to 1999)

On drinking,

"Medicine. Medicine is what it is. Bona fide cure-all. The mind is a blackboard, and this is the eraser."

The Bartender to Danny Torrance, Doctor Sleep, movie 2019, Based on the book by Stephen King

"Addiction isn't the problem, it's the solution. And until you remove the solution, you can't see clearly what the problem is."

Julie Marsden, 'Postcards from the Edge' movie 1990, based on the semi-autobiographical book by Carrie Fisher

Chapter 9
Just Geography

I'M PACKING MY suitcase and trunk for my imminent departure to London in a week's time, listening to a compilation of our favourite songs that Adam put together for me last year. The first song on Side A of the cassette tape is 'Hard to Say I'm Sorry', the lyrics burning my insides like fresh salt on raw wounds. Packing to leave home for another country sounds deceptively simple when it is anything but. It's not the possessions that matter to me, but the people, how they make me feel, and the associated memories — how do I pack those? I also wonder how I will offload the emotional baggage that won't register on any airport scales, but will weigh heavy on me as I try to move on to the next stage of my journey. I've learned the hard way that there is a price to pay for the choices I made last year; the hardest pill for me to swallow is having to let go and accept the fact that I will be far apart from everyone I care about. Six thousand, seven hundred and thirty-six miles apart to be exact.

It's been six months since I saw Adam and I remember our last conversation as if it were yesterday. "She's still watching us. I can't even …" his voice trails off into a frustrated groan and he slams his hand down on the stone seat so hard it must really hurt, but he doesn't even notice because he's so upset. I glance up towards our living room window which overlooks the pool area where we are sitting. Mum's silhouette fills the frame and she's glowering at Adam, I can feel it. I want to reach over, hold his hand, and comfort him, but I can't. We know the rules and have to abide by them, or we won't get to see each other ever again — my parents made that very clear when they issued their ultimatum.

It's our five-year anniversary and we should be celebrating with a romantic meal and some cocktails. Instead, we're being chaperoned by my Mum and sitting a metre apart, as though we've gone back two thousand years to the Zhou Dynasty, meeting for the first time with a matchmaker hosting the tea, me anxiously waiting to see if Adam will offer me the saucer with an embroidered red bag on it. But there will be no red bag, saucer acceptances, tea ceremonies or weddings. Not in the near future. Maybe not ever. We've skipped all the niceties and fast-forwarded to the part where the young couple are married and expecting their first baby. Except there is no baby. Just us, sitting next to each other, so close and yet so far apart, wishing we had made different choices.

The shrill sound of a ringing telephone interrupts my reverie and I look up to see Mum's silhouette disappearing like an apparition. Adam closes the distance between us in a split second. Now he's holding me in his arms, then lifting my tear-streaked face to kiss me, his hands roaming all over my body as if he's committing every single bone and curve to memory. Then they settle around my shoulders and he asks gently, "When did you last eat?"

"I don't know. Yesterday maybe?"

"Simone! You have got to be kidding me. You promised me you would look after yourself. You're too thin! I'm afraid to hug you in case I break you!" He lifts my wrists up, easily encircling both with one hand to show me what I already know — I'm more bone than curve. I want to tell him that it's too late, I'm already broken and you can't fix me. I want to explain that I'm so full of guilt, there isn't room for anything else. But I don't want to upset him further, so I try to lighten the mood with a feeble attempt at humour,

"I'm fine Adam. I'm sure it's just a phase. I'll grow out of it soon and then you'll regret it because I'll get so fat, you won't want me or love me anymore!"

"You know I'll always want you! I want you now." He brings my wrists down onto his lap and I can feel how aroused he is. My body instinctively responds, aching to feel fulfilled again. Our kiss deepens. But I pull away before I lose control, disgusted with myself for being addicted to him. Our bodies are so tuned into each other, he can feel my internal conflict. He sighs, "I'm sorry. I shouldn't have done that." That's all we seem to do nowadays — apologise. For everything.

"MONE!" Mum warns loudly like an angry screech owl, back at her surveillance station. Adam reluctantly releases me from the cocoon of his arms and moves a decent distance away from me. We both sigh simultaneously.

"I'm worried about you. You're so quiet all the time and even when you speak, it's like you're stuck in a tunnel, you sound really distant and far away..." He pauses, trying to find the right words.

"There's nothing to worry about. I'm quiet because I've been so preoccupied with finishing my exams. I feel exhausted most of the time. Sorry, it's just taking me a while to recover from the operation." Adam looks totally guilt-stricken, and I immediately feel bad for reminding him about the complications I suffered during the D&C procedure, where I lost a lot of blood. "It wasn't your fault, Adam. It only happens three percent of the time. I was just one of the unlucky ones. No one could have foreseen that happening."

"But it is my fault. If I hadn't made love to you, you wouldn't have ended up having the D&C, and we would be free to do what we want now, instead of this!" He throws his hands up in exasperation, slamming them back down onto the stone bench.

"I wanted you too, so it's just as much my fault as yours. But there's no point in playing the blame game Adam, because sadly, we can't go back and undo it all."

We're just going over the same old ground, stuck in a vicious circle of guilt-fuelled regret and recrimination, both unhappy when we're together but also terrified to be apart. Five years is a long time when you're a teenager, and Adam is all I've ever known. My first kiss, my first love, my first everything.

Now I find myself at another crossroads and I know I need to walk on alone. I summon what little strength I have left. "We can't go on like this anymore Adam. We're both unhappy. All I have ever wanted is for you to be happy. You need to go on without me and find happiness where you can. I still love you, but that's why I have to let you go."

"But you said you'd marry me, that we could have our own family. I know we were too young this time, but we can still have children in the future."

"I can't Adam, I'm sorry, I just can't. Because every time I look at them, I will always be mourning our first."

We sit in silence for a long while, heartbroken. Finally, Adam gets up to leave.

"Promise me you'll keep in touch, Simone. I want you to keep my ring because as far as I'm concerned, we've been married for two years and counting. I'll always be here for you. Promise me."

I nod, unable to speak. When he gets to the main road, he looks back. It takes all my strength not to run to him and retract everything I said. We look at each other for the last time, eyes full of tears and broken dreams. Then I turn away and let him go.

IT'S BEEN TWO months since I saw Adam and I am keeping myself busy with my UCCA[47] application to universities in London. Mum and Pa are arranging a loan through a rich towkay friend and I feel bad for adding to their burden because they are already financing Steph through her law degree. I worry about how they will afford the additional costs, but Mum tells me not to worry — she wants

---

47. UCCA: Universities Central Council on Admissions provided a clearing house for university applications in the UK.

to give us the university education that she never had so we can become independent and successful. I am grateful but also afraid to admit to her that she is more excited than I am; I seem to have lost the ability to get excited about anything nowadays.

I'm sitting in the library of the British Council minding my own business, replying to UCCA correspondence, when I sense someone staring at me. I look up to find myself gazing into a pair of blue-grey eyes, the colour of the sea just before a storm breaks. Mr. Blue-Grey smiles invitingly, clearly keen to engage in conversation, but I look down after giving him a shy smile. I think nothing of it, finish writing my replies, and make my way down to the café, putting my bag down to chope[48] a table before going to the counter to order some tea. As I turn from the table, Mr Blue-Grey approaches with two steaming mugs and places them on the table I've just choped. I remove my bag and sit down.

"I assumed you don't take sugar in your tea, because you look sweet enough to me.", his very English accent sends a small shiver down my spine.

"You assumed correctly."

He introduces himself, although I feel it's just a formality because we're already conversing as if we've been best friends for years. His name is Tom. Within thirty minutes, I learn that he's there because his father works at the British Council, and they met for breakfast earlier. He popped into the library to work on his application for a Master's degree in Archaeology that he'll begin next year in the UK. He's staying for a month before going to Sri Lanka for a three-month dig after two years of living in Japan. He wonders if I could spare the time to show him all the sights that Singapore has to offer, winking meaningfully. He's a shameless flirt, eight years older, romantically far more experienced than me, and exactly what I need right now — someone to distract me from my sadness.

I agree to be his guide, even though I already know he wants more than that from the cheeky twinkle in his eyes. We spend the

---

48. Chope: Singlish for reserve/book.

next three weeks discovering our shared love of reading and shared interest in learning about different cultures and their associated myths, folklore and history. He is fascinated when I recount Mama's stories, like the time when the Japanese would display the severed heads of local anti-Japanese insurgents on Merdeka Bridge to quell rebellion against their rule; also how one of Mama's cousins survived the Sook Ching[49] during which hundreds of army-age Singaporean men, including him, were forced to dig trenches on Changi Beach, before being fired on and falling dead into the graves they had just dug. We talk through the psychological impact of PTSD from lying in the open grave overnight with his dead friends — how his hair turned fully white after the trauma, and his resultant intolerance of sudden loud noises. We visit Fort Canning, browse and laugh together in bookshops, stroll through the Botanic Gardens hand in hand, explore the Fort Siloso tunnels, and swim in the lagoon at Sentosa Island, where he kisses me and tells me he's falling madly in love with me.

I am hesitant to love him because we've only just met, but I can't deny our comfortable connection that needs no words, the harmonious meeting of our minds and the strong sexual attraction between us. I tell him about Adam and how recent events have indelibly scarred me, and I am slightly surprised and more than gratified by his compassionate response and acceptance. He explains how surprised he is too about the speed at which our feelings for each other have developed, because he thought he had left his heart behind in Japan after he broke up with his girlfriend Yuka, when her family refused to accept her relationship with a foreigner. We spend his last week in Singapore exploring each other – he impresses me with his passionately gentle lovemaking, and how he takes responsibility for protecting me in a way that Adam never did.

When it's time for him to fly to Sri Lanka, Tom leaves it to the last minute to go through airport security. Even after he walks

---

49. Sook Ching: The mass killing that occurred from 18 February to 4 March 1942 in Singapore after it fell to the Japanese.

through the sliding doors, he returns to where I am standing on the other side and holds his hands up against the glass so our palms and fingers face and meet in mirrored unison. We're both reluctant to say goodbye, so instead we mouth farewell with tears in our eyes. In early November for my birthday, I receive two masks from Sri Lanka, one representing sorrow and the other joy, along with a letter from Tom telling me how much he misses and loves me, and promising to call on my birthday. He keeps his promise and is delighted to hear I have received unconditional offers from all the UK universities I applied to. We make plans to reunite in London in two months' time.

Even though my first term at university won't begin till September 1989, my parents are keen for me to leave Singapore, to put distance between Adam and me, and for me to familiarise myself with London and the UK before I start at uni. For the first time in a long time, a little frisson of excitement bubbles up inside me and I allow myself to hope for a fresh start in a different country.

I NOW UNDERSTAND what Mum meant when she complained about the bone-chilling cold of London in January, and how she couldn't bear to walk around its littered lanes because it was a million miles away from the clean, safe and well-ordered streets of Singapore, where you would be fined five hundred dollars if caught littering or spitting. Although London is more densely populated than my hometown, it feels eclectically expansive, filled to the brim with cultural diversity, and spacious enough for my sponge-like soul to decompress and expand with new connections and experiences. The tables have turned, with Tom now being my guide only a few days after meeting me at Heathrow Airport. He seems to relish his new job as tour lead and after walking from Soho and Piccadilly to Green Park, he tells me we're going to see his Auntie Liz. I feel really nervous because

I'm dressed very casually, until he marches me up to the gates at Buckingham Palace! Punching him playfully on his upper arm, we both giggle at how gullible I am.

"I trusted you!" I say in a jokingly reproachful voice.

"It was worth the little white lie just to see the surprise on your face!" he responds laughingly, trying to kiss me as I squirm away pretending to be angry, but capitulating in his arms and surrendering to his kiss almost immediately.

"Get a room, you two!" a nearby bloke teases loudly. We stop and look over sheepishly, then Tom pulls me away and starts walking down Constitution Hill towards Pall Mall and St James's Palace.

"Actually, you do need to get a room, don't you? After all, you can't stay in the guest room at College Hall much longer!" I had nine months till September to find temporary digs and a job before the start of my first term, because my meagre funds would soon run out if I continued to stay at Steph's halls of residence much longer. I would have stayed with Tom but he's squatting with friends in East London and he doesn't feel it would be appropriate accommodation for me. "We're going to meet Deuan and Bridget right after I show you a different, darker side of London — I know they're looking for a new lodger." We spend little to no time at Trafalgar Square, taking a few obligatory photos of Admiral Nelson as I can sense Tom's urgency to move on. Walking across Waterloo Bridge with the words to ABBA's hit song 'Waterloo' playing in my head, I look across at Tom and reflect on how quickly I've surrendered my heart, hoping that he will look after it with love.

We reach the underpass near the Bullring roundabout that will take us to Waterloo station. As we descend down the ramp, my eyes adjusting to the darkness, I hear low groans, pained grunts and unsettling noises. I grip Tom's hand tighter. "Welcome to London's Cardboard City!" he whispers dramatically, revealing the distressing scene before us with a sombre sweep of his left hand. All around us, they lie huddled on makeshift mattresses

made out of cardboard and tattered rags, emaciated and skeletal with sallow skin, mouths stretched open in broken-toothed grimaces; one of them reaches out her crow-like claw, croaking hoarsely at me, "Can you spare some change, love?" Here they lie, surrounded by the stench of cheap alcohol, urine and excrement, London's lonely, its homeless — destitute, uncared for and forgotten. I give her all the money I have in my purse, squeezing her bony hand gently, tears falling now because I can feel her unspoken despair and desperation, wondering how the hell she fell so far from grace.

#

THE RELENTLESS PACE of city life is something both London and Singapore have in common. Within a month, I've found a temporary job in telesales after applying to a two-line advert in the Evening Standard. I rush round Chinatown gathering up ingredients to cook a special Valentine's Day dinner for Tom, after a long day making cold calls to sell luxury hotel memberships in dream destinations like the Maldives. I seem to have inherited Pa's ability to sell ice to the Eskimos, making enough money in my first month to pay for three months' rent, and giving any spare cash to my homeless friends at Cardboard City.

I went back the day after Tom took me there, bringing some homemade soup that I rustled up in Steph's student hall kitchen. I found Frances again, heartbroken by her sad story of how she was abandoned by her boyfriend when she was pregnant at sixteen, was forced to have an abortion by her parents, could find no other means of surviving except prostitution when she left home in search of a better life in London, and is now addicted to heroin after her pimp introduced it as a recreational drug, but really to keep her under his control. Frances is a year younger than me at eighteen even though she looks ten years older, and I shudder to think how that could so easily be me in her shoes.

Dinner's now ready, Tom knocks on the door of our four bedroom flat in Balham and I rush downstairs to the front door to let him in. It's been two weeks since we last spent time together and he felt far away then. Tonight, we have the flat all to ourselves because Deuan and Bridget are out, so I'm hoping we can talk. I can tell something's wrong as soon as I look into his eyes, but he looks away, then studiously avoids further eye contact while we're eating. After dinner, he holds me tight and kisses me with such sad longing that I pull away and ask him to tell me what is going on.

"I wish we could stay like this forever. If only we'd met years ago before I went to Japan, things would be so different. I've been trying to tell you for weeks, but I selfishly wanted you all to myself. Besides, I don't know how long she's staying so I kept hoping you wouldn't find out till after she's gone home. I'm just so torn between doing what's right by her and doing what I want to do — to be with you!"

"Tom, who are you talking about? I'm confused. Is…is it Yuka? Is she here in London now?" He nods, unable to answer. He eventually confesses that after exchanging letters in the months after he left Japan, she surprised him in London two weeks after I landed and is now staying at the squat with him.

"So, for the last month, you've been sleeping with both of us?"

He nods. "I know it's looks bad but I was with her for two years and we weren't together anymore when you and I met. I've never felt about anyone the way I feel for you, Simone. Even when I was in Sri Lanka, I felt connected to you here." He points to his heart. "It's like I could hear your voice even though we were thousands of miles apart, I could hear your thoughts. The last time we made love, I tried to distance myself mentally to see if I could stand to be apart from you, and I can't. That's why I'm here now."

"What do you want from me, Tom?"

"I want everything. But I can't tell Yuka yet. Not after she's come all this way."

I imagine how I would feel if I were Yuka and Tom's telling me how he's met the love of his life, how he wants to be with her after just five months. I imagine the hurt, anger and betrayal bubbling up inside her. I hear myself talking things through with Tom in autopilot. It's like the real me has checked out and gone somewhere else, leaving in her place a highly logical android devoid of emotion and able to make sensible decisions. I hear Android Me tell Tom that he should stay faithful to Yuka and that we can be just friends. If and when Yuka leaves to go home, we can rekindle our romantic relationship because I know I will still love him. I make it so easy for Tom, he almost smiles as he leaves to go after giving me a wistfully long goodbye kiss.

As I shut the front door, the shutters come down inside, locking away the grief from this latest loss. I wanted to beg Tom to stay, to come clean with Yuka and tell her that he's met his soul mate, I wanted him to fight for me. But I said nothing because I knew it was too good to be true, that after everything I've done, I don't deserve to be happy. Mum once told me how she knew that God had finally forgiven her for sinning with the abortion — Sacred Heart Jesus appeared in her dream blessing her with his hands, then shortly afterwards, she found out she was pregnant with Steph. I would love to believe that such heavenly forgiveness would extend to me too, because it doesn't feel like God wants me to be happy; it doesn't feel like he even exists.

Tom is gone, leaving me with that familiar feeling of not being enough. It's the same story of sorrowful loss and the same sad me, just in a different country.

Chapter 5
The Lost Years

Losing My Religion: How Alcohol becomes my Best Buddy

"Go on Mone, go on, you can do it!"

Pa encourages me in an excitedly loud voice because he stands to win fifty dollars from God-Pa Bernard if I down this glass of brandy before my god-cousin David does. I drink it all down first, with ease, and God-Pa Bernard grudgingly hands over the money to a jubilant Pa. It's become a yearly tradition every Christmas since I was eight years old and marks the start of my complicated relationship with alcohol. From as far back as I can remember, drinking was woven into the fabric of our lives — at multiple weddings where the bride and groom were being toasted with loud cheers of Yam-seng[50], at home with bottles of beers chilling in the fridge and brandy on the table, at family get-togethers sampling whiskeys from around the world, and at every Ang-moh customer dinner Pa made us attend.

#

---

50. Yam-seng: Hokkien for bottoms up/cheers, literally translated as 'drink to victory'.

In London, going to the pub is more commonplace than going to the gym. I wonder what it will be like when I get to Oxford as I flick through my dog-eared copy of Jane Eyre. I'm at the part when Rochester, now nearly blind, is pining for Jane at Ferndean Manor. I'm excited to catch up with Mave, who is studying at Exeter College, one of the many colleges at the University of Oxford. The coach has been stopping to pick up passengers since I got on at Victoria, where it began its journey. I hear the bus driver exclaim with barely concealed impatience, "Come on mate, are you getting on or not?!" I look up to see a rather tall, dark-haired gentleman holding up the entire queue behind him. He's staring at me with barely concealed curiosity, fixated even, rooted to the spot. The passengers behind him are getting restless and some of them mutter impatiently at him to "Hurry up, will you!". He takes his time, unperturbed by the levels of irritation around him. He walks to the table seat I'm sitting at, stops and asks very politely, "If no one is sitting here, please may I join you?" He sounds extremely European — grammatically perfect English with every syllable crisply enunciated in a rather formal manner.

"Yes of course, please do." I'm slightly perplexed as to why he's chosen the seat across from me, having walked past several vacant seats on his way over. He immediately engages in conversation and tells me he's meeting up with old friends for a reunion after graduating two years ago. I explain that I'm looking forward to spending time with my best friend from Singapore who is reading Jurisprudence (law) at Oxford Uni. His name is Till, his father is German and his mum Italian; he speaks six languages fluently and he's the youngest Marketing Manager at Visa, as well as a part-time model for Giorgio Armani and other luxury brands. It's all very impressive, but I'm more taken with how he listens attentively and the books he reads — we share a love of 'The Alchemist' and 'One Hundred Years of Solitude', indicating that Till is a kindred spirit.

When we both get off the coach at Oxford City Centre, he insists on walking me to the porter house at Exeter College. It's out of his way but the gentleman in him wants to ensure my safety. We exchange telephone numbers and agree to meet in London sometime soon. Later that night after meeting Mave, I find out in the student bar at Exeter College that everyone in Oxford (apart from nerdy Asians) loves to drink. Pa's Christmas drink training comes in handy, enabling me to win numerous drinking games throughout the night, despite being the smallest in stature. Very drunk but still standing at midnight, my mind returns to my conversation with Adam earlier today.

"I MISS YOU. I can't stop thinking about you. What are you doing right now? When are you coming home?" He asks me questions that I can't answer without hurting him.

"I don't know Adam. I'm just playing it by ear — I haven't decided when I'll return." *Or even if I will return*, I think silently. "I'm working and saving money right now before I start uni in September."

"Have you met someone else?"

I pause before answering his question, debating whether I should tell him about Tom but that's over, so "No, I'm single. I'm not sure Fate likes me very much — I don't seem to be very lucky in love. What about you?"

"Well, I'm dating someone but she's a bit of an Ah Lian, so it won't go very far. Besides, my heart already belongs to someone else."

"Oh, and who might that be?" I ask hopefully while trying to suppress the sharp sting of jealousy at the thought of him moving on, even though I had asked him to.

"You know my heart belongs to you. If you promise to come back during your holidays, I'll break up with her and wait for you to finish your degree. I might even be able to save enough money to come see you at Christmas time and we can celebrate my birthday in London without your parents knowing."

Tempting as it is to fall back into old ways and as much as I miss him, I know that horse has already bolted, so the gate needs shutting once and for all, "I can't make you any promises Adam. Please let me go and be happy. I'm really sorry."

#

Till calls me on Monday evening and we agree to meet up in Soho on Friday night. After a manic but successful day at work, I make it to the bar ten minutes late, all flushed, flustered and apologetic. His manners are impeccable; he stands as soon as I arrive, pulls out my chair and ensures I'm seated comfortably before he sits down again. I notice the single ladies at the bar swooning over all six feet and three inches of him. I can see why — with his dark hair falling in loose waves to his chin, glasses framing his long-lashed green eyes, his chiselled jawline and a physique so athletic it would put Adonis to shame.

We've sunk about six cocktails each and are so engrossed in conversation about Kafka, that neither of us notices the guy with a bucket of individually wrapped red roses thrusting his wares on the table. Eventually, I look up and say no thank you, but Till pulls him to one side and a few minutes later, returns to our table with all the roses in his arms. I hear irritated sighs from the single ladies nearby and feel sure I would now be dead if looks could kill. I thank Till for such extravagant generosity, feeling bad that he spent so much money on me. He leans in for a kiss and I feel even worse during and after it, because there's no reciprocal passion — there are no birds singing or bells ringing! I just feel overwhelming gratitude for the gift of meeting such a perfect person, someone too good to be true, whose love I am simply not worthy of.

Till and I continue to meet every weekend and talk almost every evening. He is in every way the archetypal Prince Charming who only exists in fairy tales or romance novels. I can't understand why he's still around when we haven't done anything more than kiss. I persevere with our relationship even though there is no spark on my side, because he's finally found a companion he can confide in, especially in crowded-yet-lonely London, and I don't want to let him down. I get the impression he thinks I can do no wrong. I don't want to burst his bubble, so I say nothing about Adam, the baby I still mourn or my sordid past.

At the end of May he surprises me with a travel proposal, asking me to accompany him on an all-expenses-paid European trip over July and August, mixing business with pleasure, sleeping in separate rooms in luxury hotels, no strings attached. It's the opportunity of a lifetime, but I can't continue with the charade of keeping up appearances and pretending to be perfect when I am fundamentally flawed. So I turn him down as gently as I can,

"Thank you so much Till — I'm really grateful for your generosity. I'm truly sorry, but I have to work over the summer. Please go have lots of fun and I'll see you when you get back." He tries his best to change my mind, but concedes to my stubbornness after a few days. He promises to write me a postcard every day in one of the six languages he speaks. True to his word, I receive little love missives from Till every day while he's away, professing his undying love (ti voglio bene, te amo, ich liebe dich, je t'aime, eu te amo, I love you[51]). But I know he doesn't love the real (hidden) me, just the idea of perfect me, the one who doesn't exist.

#

Tom and Deuan go back a long way, back to their days in Uni over a decade ago. So it doesn't surprise me when Tom starts to call me more often after a few weeks of Till's love-filled postcards. Yuka is still in London and I've seen how she clings to him at parties we've all been to, so I think I made the right decision in February, even though it still hurts and I miss Mr Blue-Grey very much. Life goes on regardless — I just focus on putting one

---

51. I love you in Italian, Spanish, German, French, Portuguese and English.

foot in front of the other, trying hard not to think too far ahead.

I'm on my way to Cardboard City for my weekly Saturday meal with Frances, her favourite chicken chow mein still warm in the thermal bag I'm carrying. I've been trying my best to cheer her up over the last few months, but she's sliding deeper and deeper into the abyss, and I'm afraid I can't save her no matter how hard I try. I share her guilt-fuelled feelings of hopelessness, deep regret and sorrow. I know how much she hates and blames herself for the poor choices she's made. I know she drinks herself into a stupor and shoots up to numb the pain, holding off the anxiety for just a little bit longer. How it's easier to feel nothing than to feel so much your heart breaks with the weight of too much emotion. I know she's so paralysed by pain that she can't break away from the vicious vortex of despair that's pulling her down into the abyss — the darkness that knows her name and whispers it incessantly, welcoming her to stay forever where she will feel nothing.

I look around for Frances because her cardboard 'coffin' is empty — that's what we jokingly nickname the small, cramped space she's usually slumped in. I walk along the length of the underpass, round the corner and to the other side, calling her name, but no one answers. A small seed of panic begins to unfurl from deep down inside me, I walk faster, back the way I came, calling out her name more frantically now, "Frances, Frances, where are you? Frances, please answer me! FRANCES!" One of my other street friends waves me over. He's a young lad but like Frances, looks ten years older than he is, frown lines indelibly etched into his craggy face, so he always looks upset and angry. He slurs softly, I only catch the name Frances, so I beg him to repeat what he said as I kneel on the grime-blackened concrete next to him. He holds out his hand instinctively, always on the look-out for his next fix. Hurriedly, I press a ten-pound note into his hand while asking him to please tell me where Frances is.

"Dey took 'er away yest'day. In da night. Dere woz all dis white shit foamin' out her mouf and her eyes woz open. But she wern dere. She wern dere. She da lucky one, dat Frances. Da lucky one." He's half cackling, half crying, as he says the words I am dreading, "She dead."

I'M SITTING WITH my head in my hands, eyes closed in a vain attempt to blot out the images of my poor, dead Frances being zipped up in a black body bag after she overdosed, then dumped and buried in a grave with two other nameless souls, no prayers uttered or hymns sung for her soul's salvation at her pauper's funeral. At the local Police station, I try to ask where her body is, but no one cares enough to find out, so I leave after a few hours. I can't even say goodbye. There's no one home with me, they're all out partying on a Saturday night. And even if they were here, I know I wouldn't say anything, because nothing I say will bring her back, there's nothing I can do or say to bring back everyone I've lost.

I hear someone insistently knocking on our front door and open it to find Tom standing there. He wipes away the tears from my eyes, pulls me into his arms, and holds me until I stop sobbing. "You called?" I can't believe how, after all this time, he can still hear my thoughts when we're apart. Then we're kissing, making up for lost time, even though Conscience is screaming at me to stop. All those long months of restraint and denial are evaporating as rapidly as searing hot steam from an active volcano after lying dormant for years. We're so desperate to feel whole again that we barely make it upstairs. Tom half carries, half pulls me into my room, our need for each other so urgent that we don't even bother getting undressed. We spend the night wrapped around each other in my tiny single bed, no words needed, saving all the guilty recriminations for the cold light of day.

Tom leaves in the early morning so he can get home without having to explain his whereabouts to Yuka. Before he goes, we both apologise for having lost control. I picture Yuka's face if she ever finds out, and I'm immediately consumed by guilt, remembering Mama's advice to always treat others as we would like to be treated. Guilt, when compounded and bottled up inside, becomes this hard, flinty gouge, digging and excavating until there's nothing left but a bottomless void. No matter how much alcohol I drink, nothing fills it. But at least it takes the edge off the pain, dulling its sharp serrations till I can almost bear it. Drinking blurs my mind and memories, making it easier for me to pretend that I've been living in a waking nightmare. It's how I cope.

It's the end of August and I leave for university in five days' time. We're all at our local, The Bedford, about half an hour's walk from where we live. Deuan and Bridget are leaving shortly for a party in Brixton but I decline the invitation to join them, because I know Tom will be there with Yuka and I can't handle another massive guilt trip right now. I know most of the locals anyway, from sharing daily after-work pints and weekend binge-drinking. Everyone's buying me a farewell drink and I have about seven or eight pints of Snakebite in quick succession before last orders are called at 11pm. One of the locals, Chris, a minicab driver in his twenties, whose girlfriend I talk to frequently when commuting to work, invites me to a party in Streatham. He tells me that Chanel will be there too after she finishes her late-night shift. Chris has been on soft drinks, having just stopped his shift, so is safe to drive us to the party.

Chris, his friend Mike and I are singing in his minicab on the way to Streatham. Caron Wheeler's husky voice is mesmerising in the residual summer heat as she asks provocatively, "How ever do you want me, how ever do you need me …" I can see why this song held the coveted number 1 spot in the UK

Singles Chart for four weeks this summer, the heart-poundingly rhythmic bass accentuating Soul II Soul's sensual sounds. Mike likes it so much he keeps rewinding it, so it's the only song we sing along to for the entire journey, but I don't mind as we're all in the mood for a party.

When we get to the house, I'm surprised to find that there's only one other person there — Scott, the host, who assures me that others are on their way, pubs are only just chucking people out so he's expecting everyone else to turn up after midnight. I feel slightly uneasy, but Scott puts 'Back to Life' on full blast and hands me a rum and coke. The music is so loud, I can feel the bass thumping through the walls as I take a large gulp of my drink. Scott's been very generous with the Captain Morgan's, I can feel it burning all the way down my throat even though I'm used to drinking brandy and whiskey neat from Pa's Christmas drinking games. Mike grabs my hands and pulls me to my feet for a dance, grinding his hips against mine suggestively. I pull away and take another gulp, suddenly feeling slightly nervous. "Hey girl, come on and move your body, show us what you've got, we wanna see that ass swaying to the beat." He grabs my hips from behind when I turn away to sit down on an armchair across from the sofa and pulls me firmly onto his lap while Chris and Scott make whooping noises of appreciation at the way Mike is showing me who's boss.

"No, please stop! I really don't feel like dancing." I feel extremely light-headed and the walls of the room appear to be pulsating, zooming in and out of focus. "Chris, please can you just take me home now, I feel like I'm going to be sick!" My voice sounds funny, very distant, and the thumping music has faded into the background as if someone's put mufflers over the speakers; everything looks and feels elongated and misshapen like the melting clocks in a Salvador Dali painting.

Chris's voice has changed. He sounds stern like a headteacher who's about to cane me for spoiling his fun, "We're not going anywhere! We only just got here. You need to lighten up and relax. Yo Scott, you got any more of that Vitamin K? Get it down her neck so we can all go to K-land." Scott approaches me with more rum and coke, and sprinkles what looks like refined sugar into my drink. All my muscles have stopped obeying me — they feel strangely relaxed. I will my head to shake no, but nothing happens. Scott sits next to me and pours the drink down my throat in one go. It tastes like rum but makes me feel so odd, like I have the body of a rag doll.

"I need to go to the loo." Mike grunts as Scott pulls me up off his lap and takes me downstairs to a dark bedroom with an ensuite bathroom. I can see light shining through the slightly open door. Thankfully, he stays outside while I pee quickly, then splash cold water over my face, already feeling very sober but trying to shake off the heavy inertia weighing down my disobedient limbs. I hear voices outside the door, it sounds like they're arguing — "I get to go on the ride first, you wanker! I drew the longest straw, then Chris, which means you're up last!" Maybe some other people have turned up to join the party, which is good because my body feels like someone else's now, and I could really do with a lie down.

I pull the door towards me tentatively, the bedroom is now in semi-darkness because I can make out the halo surrounding a lamp on the bedside table. The lamp looks alive, the halo circling over it like a buzzard stalking its prey. Scott's gone and Mike is standing right in front of me, blocking out most of the light from the halo-lamp. He grabs me and throws me face down onto the bed, his hand holding me by my hair and pulling my head back towards him while his other hand pulls off my skirt and underwear in one practised movement, I manage a strangled "No!" but he ignores it, slams my head back down into the mattress to muffle my screams, and tells me to enjoy the ride.

Hours later, there's birdsong and I hear Chris saying it's time to go. Autopilot Me gets up, gets dressed and gets into his minicab. He's chatting cheerfully about something inane, making small talk, while I sit in silence, feeling dirty and defiled. Some time later, he drops me off at my front door. I hear him shout out, "See you around!" and then he pulls away without a care in the world.

I spend the next hour sitting slumped in the shower, scrubbing myself clean until everything is red-raw. For the briefest moment, I think about reporting the rape, but dismiss the thought as soon as I think it. I can hear the objections now — her skirt was too short; she was drunk and asking for it; she only said no to tease us. I know I should seek justice to prevent this from happening to someone else, but I just haven't got it in me to deal with all the stress and shame if I blow the whistle. I haven't cried once through the whole ordeal because I am furious with myself for being so naive and trusting, and ashamed of how I've allowed alcohol to override Common Sense, running riot with my life and taking over it.

I visit the out-of-hours GP later that day to ask for the morning-after pill. I explain how I would also like a urine test because I suspect I was drugged last night. The GP looks overworked, tired and fed up because he's working over the long weekend. He accedes to my request and tells me to contact my own GP after the bank holiday to get the results. On Tuesday, I walk into a sexual health clinic in Wandsworth for a full check-up to ensure I haven't picked up any STIs. On Thursday, the day before I move to New Orchard Hall at Westfield College, my GP calls to ask if I've had a prescription from a private psychiatrist to treat depression. I say no and ask why.

"Well, that's odd because we found high levels of ketamine in your urine sample. My wife's a psychiatrist and she tells me it's primarily used as an experimental drug to treat chronic depression in the States, so we're wondering how it ended up in your bloodstream."

So that's why he called it Vitamin K.

Comfortably Numb: Burying my Painful Past

TWO WEEKS LATER, while other first-years are enjoying Freshers' Week, I return to Wandsworth for the results of the blood, swab and urine tests and they give me the all-clear. I'm grateful for small mercies although to be quite honest, I wish it had never happened at all. On my way back to Hampstead, I decide to bury my past, everything up till now, because I can't carry on limping through life like this. I visualise every single painful memory, imagine I am writing it down, then picture myself placing each memory note into a hand-carved wooden box that I lock with an ornate key. I bury the box filled with my guilt, regrets and shame deep inside my mind, determined not to open it unless absolutely necessary. I store the key in my heart for the day the real Prince Charming proves with his kiss that he can love me exactly as I am, that I am enough.

I decide to keep in touch with Bridget and Deuan, but not Tom or Till. I meet Till for the last time two weeks later, and he understands why we can't see each other when I explain that all this time, I've been mute like Meme (in 'One Hundred Years of Solitude'), after she arrives at the convent before giving birth to her illegitimate son Aureliano — the trauma of her painful past rendering her speechless. I would far rather he remembers me with fondness, than lives with me in disappointment. I don't say goodbye to Tom, I don't say anything at all. I just leave things between us exactly as they are.

Life on campus in the leafy London suburb of Hampstead is like a dichotomy between the Bourgeoisie and the Proletariat: we are fifteen minutes' walk away from the really rich in Hampstead with their Porsches and SUVs that never get driven off-road; in the opposite direction are those who struggle to make ends meet in West Hampstead and Kilburn, who don't own a car, walk everywhere, and only use public transport when they can afford it. There are occasional glimpses of the extraordinary — we get to wash the windscreen of George Michael's 911 during Rags & Charities week, when he drives down Kidderpore Avenue on the way to his Mum's, and we often bump into Harry Enfield when he's walking his dog. For the Drama modules of my joint Honours degree, I'm studying at Central School of Speech and Drama which boasts, among its alumni, Laurence Olivier, Judi Dench, Dawn French and Jennifer Saunders. The kiasu Singaporean in me feels slightly cowed to be associated with such illustrious company, afraid that I will disappoint with my mediocrity. I steer clear of men, preferring to surround myself with strong, like-minded female friends — Jen and Delyth who are both studying French and Drama, and Sarah who has chosen History of Art.

I soon realise that being a student is synonymous with being drunk and/or stoned, breaking the rules, and having a good time without over-thinking. One of our teachers regularly lights up a spliff when we congregate in his room for tutorials. He says it helps his creative flow. Before I know it, all my resolutions of staying sober and drug-free fly completely out of the window, and I start to experiment with cannabis and marijuana. I enjoy the feeling of numb detachment that comes with being so drunk-stoned, all I can do is lie in bed listening to music while looking at the starry night sky. By day, I manage to function on three or four hours of sleep, attending various lectures and tutorials across two locations; by night, I'm listening to Pink Floyd's 'Comfortably Numb' and 'Wish You Were Here', wistfully wishing things had

turned out differently, but thankful that my demons are locked away and buried deep in that box in my mind.

Sometime in spring 1990, I meet Simon. He is sitting on the edge of the Student Union hall stage, pint of beer in one hand and fag in the other, minding his own business, watching everyone else dance. I recognise that look of abject loneliness on his face, which compels me to walk over and say hi. Snap's number 1 hit 'The Power' is blaring loudly through the massive speakers, so we decide to go outside where we can hear ourselves think. He tells me his life story: from how he's been unemployed despite having graduated with a degree in French and German to how he is living on his own and on meagre state benefits. He's been depressed since his ex broke up with him after her affair with his then best friend. She still has a final year to finish before graduating; he sometimes comes back so he can see her and reminisce about better days. Tonight was one of those times.

At the end of our conversation, the music switches to soft and slow and he asks me to dance while Sinead O'Connor sings sorrowfully about how "Nothing Compares to You". I empathise with Simon's feelings of loss and feel his pain.

Simon and I have many intellectually stimulating conversations over the next few weeks, discovering a shared love of Kafka. He gradually becomes a part of our friendship group, spending every evening in my room instead of going back to his cheerless bedsit. I eventually help him to find and apply for a job at the Halifax Building Society as a mortgage administrator, a total waste of his linguistic talents, but much better than being on benefits. We don't have a particularly passionate relationship, but we understand each other, and enjoy being together. We're comfortable.

In a blink of an eye, I'm in my final year at Westfield and missing Jen and Deli, who are living in France for their sandwich year. Simon and I rent a small, freezing-cold, one-bedroom ground floor flat in West Hampstead, which is four doors and a road down from Unwins, the off-licence where I work in the evenings and a fifteen-minute walk to campus.

When my final term ends in June 1992, my student visa will expire and I will need to go home to Singapore. By now, Simon knows about the skeletons in my closet and is not keen for me to return home, fearing an inevitable reunion with Adam. We don't discuss it, instead focusing on his skeletons, which include his parents' acrimonious divorce (he stayed with his dad while his brother went to live with his mum and her new partner), his dad's struggle with alcohol addiction where he would consume a bottle of vodka by lunchtime, eventually ending up in hospital with Delirium Tremens, and his fear of becoming his father's son.

For Christmas and to welcome 1992, Simon plans a trip to Paris so I can meet up with Jen and Deli and make the pilgrimage to Jim Morrison's tomb in Père Lachaise cemetery. On New Year's Eve he persuades me to overcome my fear of heights and I find myself clinging (petrified) to the railing at the top of the Eiffel Tower, where he proposes we get married so I can stay in England instead of returning to Singapore. I accept, even though I still feel haunted about how it ended with Adam. I resolve my inner conflict by reminding myself that I have locked away my past in order to move on.

JUST AFTER OUR trip to Paris, my manager at Unwins increasingly leaves me alone to look after the shop in the evenings because he's trying to save his failing marriage after his wife confesses to having an affair. I feel for their three young children with their hang-dog expressions and haunted eyes, eyes that have witnessed too much domestic discord too soon. One Sunday evening, a dodgy-looking guy tries to buy just under fifty pounds' worth of alcohol with what I suspect to be a stolen credit card. When I ring to authorise the credit card transaction after pressing the silent alarm button, he attacks me, wrenching my shoulder and pulling out half my hair when he drags me across the shop, slamming me into one of the product displays. There follows a frantic car chase down Fortune Green Road towards West Hampstead train station, like something out of a Starsky & Hutch episode! The suspect is eventually apprehended after he breaks his leg trying to evade the police; he bolts out of the escape vehicle and jumps over the bridge forty feet down onto the train tracks. I spend most of January and February at the Police Station at identity parades and meeting with the Crown Prosecution Service, who have decided to file ABH (Actual Bodily Harm) charges, in addition to prosecuting him for theft and fraud. The defendant's legal aid team do their best to delay the court case in the hope that I will drop out of the lengthily painful process.

Despite this disruption, I am focused on revising for my final examinations — eighteen written papers in total. Simon is keen for us to marry before my student visa expires at the end of June, so on 8th May 1992, surrounded by his estranged parents, their new partners, his brother, Sarah (because Jen and Deli are still in France), and my cousin Ginny to represent my family, we marry in Preston registry office. After a budget weekend honeymoon break in nearby Blackpool, I return to my usual work and revision schedule. The court date is eventually set for the first two weeks in June, which coincides with my final exams. I honour my commitment to appear at Crown Court as the Prosecution's (only) star witness, deferring my finals to the following year in order to testify and prevent him from committing further crimes. The jury votes unanimously to convict and he tries again to attack me when he gets sent down for the maximum of five years in prison. I discover that there is a woeful lack of support for victims of violent crime when there is no follow-up counselling or compensation for time off, just payment to cover my travel costs.

In true Asian fashion, I get on with it and find a job recruiting social workers, taking three weeks of annual leave in June 1993 to finish my final exams and complete my degree. Simon and I spend the first year as a married couple sharing a rented flat with Sarah and her boyfriend Paul, then we buy our own freehold house in Tooting, a stone's throw away from where I used to live in Balham. We're coasting along, seemingly fine, but despite achieving promotion at work, I still suffer from imposter syndrome, wondering when someone will unveil the cloak of addiction masking my anxiety and feelings of inadequacy. Simon struggles with an inability to make positive changes in his life, instead preferring to live in despair and complain about being unhappy. We drink to forget, mired separately in our own ever-decreasing circles of discontent.

After a trip home to Singapore at Christmas, when Adam tells me that he too is married and returns the mementos of our past, I decide to walk away from my marriage to Simon, because I can only see myself sliding further down the slippery slope into more sadness and dragging him down with me. On 8th May 1994, a mere two years after we first tied the knot, I sign over the house to Simon, despite being advised against it by his lawyers, and walk away with nothing but the clothes on my back and in my suitcase.

Interlude 2

As you join me on my journey, please take a musical break and listen to the song that captures the mood of that particular moment in time. Or read on.

The choice is yours.

'Boulevard of Broken Dreams', *song from the album 'American Idiot' by Green Day, released November 2004*

Chapter 6
How to Save a Life

I MISS MAMA'S physical presence but I still see her in my memories and sense her supportive presence all the time. During the mid-Autumn (Moon) Festival, I recall her recounting the legend of how the Emperor of Heaven decides to test the virtues of three forest animals: a fox, a monkey, and a rabbit. Disguised as an old man, he descends to Earth, approaching the three animals, telling them that he is starving and asking them to find him food. The fox offers a fish after catching it in a nearby stream, while the monkey brings foraged fruit; the rabbit only has her babies to offer. When the old man has finished eating the offerings from the fox and the monkey, the rabbit tells him that he can eat her instead and jumps into the fire. To honour the rabbit's self-sacrifice, the Emperor of Heaven takes her bones to the Moon Palace, where she will be honoured for eternity. Mama explains how selflessness is at the heart of Yin, the feminine half of Yin Yang symbolised by the Moon, and how mothers in particular epitomise love through the sacrifices they make for their children. Mama urges me to always appreciate my Mum for sacrificing her own happiness by staying in an unhappy marriage to provide financial security and stability for Steph and me.

I remember watching 'The Goddess' (神女 shén nǚ) with Mama and Mum, a silent movie which moves me to tears with its tragic ending. We empathise with how the young female protagonist is forced into a sordid life of prostitution in 1930s Shanghai, in order to provide for her baby son. It's heart-breaking to see how she is exploited by her 'Boss' (a pimp with a gambling addiction) and shunned by the parents of other children in the private school she pays for her son to attend, from which he is later expelled when they discover she is a prostitute. We feel the unjustness of the situation when she is sentenced to twelve years in prison after accidentally killing her 'Boss', during an argument where she discovers he's stolen all the money she's saved to start a new life in another city. The school principal, who tried to prevent her son's expulsion, eventually ends up adopting him from the orphanage. She begs him to tell her son that his mother is dead, in order to shield him from further shame and to protect his future. This silent film speaks volumes and is made even more poignant because the actress who portrays the goddess, Ruan Lingyu, committed suicide the year after its release aged twenty-four, to escape the pain of being hounded by the press with their relentless criticism of her failed personal relationships and the "fearful gossip" that followed.

For an hour afterwards, Mum bemoans the wickedness of men, the dangers of overrated love, and extols the virtues of women, especially selfless mothers.

IT'S AFTER WORK and I pop into The Mitre pub for a quick pint before driving home for a bottle of wine with dinner for one in my rented one-bedroom flat. I hear from locals in the pub about the tragic death of a local mum (while eight months pregnant) from an epileptic fit. Doctors tried unsuccessfully to revive her and to save her unborn daughter, performing an emergency C-section after someone thought they heard the baby's heartbeat, but it was too late — both mum and baby perished, leaving behind her teenage son from a previous relationship and her grieving boyfriend Dave. I have only met Dave in passing before, but I notice he is drowning his sorrows; looks like he's been in the pub since it opened at 12 noon. I notice him ignoring an older lady (presumably his mum), her left leg in a cast and boot, as she repeatedly tries to get him to leave. She appeals to some of the regulars for help to get him home to Balham, but no one steps up. I take my now-empty glass to the bar and leave, but something (fate maybe?) makes me turn back and I hear myself offering Mary and her very drunk son Dave a lift home to Balham. She is unable to bear much weight because of her replacement knee, so I end up having to shoulder most of Dave's weight, because he is legless[52]!

I stay till late, listening to Mary offload her worries and frustrations over a few bottles of Chardonnay in the lounge, while Dave snores loudly in her front bedroom. I learn that he is the middle child of her estranged marriage to a Korean War veteran of American-German descent. How Herb swept her off her feet in London in the late 1950s. How she spent most of the sixties travelling to and from Indiana, unable to settle in the States, enduring much unhappiness and violence when Herb lost his patience with her habitual homesickness, often flying into jealous rages about her flirting with other men while working as a nightclub photographer. She explains how she had to lie to her parents about her firstborn's birth date, pretending she was born in September rather than June, to hide the fact that she was pregnant before their shotgun wedding. Dave has grown up without knowing his father (she left America for good when he was three), but he exhibits the same worrying proclivity for occasionally violent outbursts of anger. Aged thirty-four (nearly ten years older than me), he's been drifting in and out of trouble all his life, eventually leaving the special school he was sent to (for badly behaved boys) with only one O 'Level — a grade D in English. She appeals to me for help and asks me to be the

---

52. Legless: British slang for being so drunk, one has lost control of their legs and can't walk.

friend Dave so desperately needs.

I feel for them both and spend the next few months sharing the burden of care. Mary's lack of mobility hampers her daily activities, so I do all of their shopping, cleaning, cooking and laundry. I pay for food and bills to supplement Dave's dole money because he's too depressed to work right now. Dave lives three doors up from Mary in a maisonette overlooking Tooting Bec common, a few streets down from the place I rent, and I help him move back into his flat from his late girlfriend's home. Mary and I take turns at suicide watch, because apparently, Dave tried to kill himself by running out in front of traffic when he was drunk, not long after the funeral.

Because I work during the week, Mary and I agree it would make more sense for me to take the night shift. I start off by sleeping in Dave's spare bedroom, waking up several times during the night to check on him as a mother would check on her new born baby, thankful that I'm able to function on only three to four hours of broken sleep — a habit formed not long after my eighteenth birthday.

A few weeks before Christmas, during our usual Friday night binge-drinking session and before Dave becomes incoherent from alcohol, he admits that he is afraid I will leave him when I find out what a bad man he really is. The truth rushes out in a torrent of guilt-driven confession as if I am a Catholic priest in the confession booth at church, able to absolve him of all sins. I listen to him sharing how he thinks his actions caused the deaths of his girlfriend and their baby. Their complicated ten-year relationship started not long after his ex-wife left him with nothing but a bag of peas in the chest freezer that was too bulky for her to move (she took everything else). His girlfriend had a toddler from a previous relationship and insisted on her son having regular contact with his biological father, even though he didn't pay a penny towards his child's upbringing — something she and Dave argued a lot about, even coming to blows on a few occasions. She was an epileptic and despite taking drugs for the condition, would experience several fits a month. She lived for her son, putting him before anyone else including Dave, but he didn't care as long as she was there to cook, clean and provide sex when he needed it.

Dave became increasingly frustrated during the last few years of their relationship when she began questioning the nights he spent away from her, when she put pressure on him to have a child so she could have someone to love, now that her son was growing up. He didn't dare confirm her suspicions that he'd been having casual sex and one-night stands for years, until after a lads-only holiday to Ibiza when he fell for a much younger twenty-year-old. He carried on the affair for months while they were trying for a baby, and was forced to make a choice by his girlfriend when she caught them canoodling on the common, just after she told him she was pregnant. He chose the younger model because she was a much better 'shag'[53], but had gone back to his girlfriend a month before her death, after the new 'sort'[54] tired of him and began sleeping with guys her own age.

The night she died, he'd left her and her son because he was too irritated by their bickering, and went to his mum's to get away for the night. He didn't rush back until he received a distress call from her son panicking about being unable to wake her, but it was too late to save her. The autopsy revealed extensive oesophageal damage, identifying the cause of death as asphyxiation from blocked airways after Vicky had vomited during the epileptic seizure. The coroner concluded that she had been suffering for quite a while with bulimia. Dave recalls her always visiting the bathroom after meals, and her confessed fear of him leaving her for a much slimmer and better-looking girl, a fear that he made real with his actions leading up to her demise.

While I don't approve of Dave's choices or his disloyalty, how he doesn't distinguish between sex and making love, and how badly he treated his girlfriend, I see how genuinely sorry he

---

53. Shag: noun - the act of sexual intercourse; verb - to have sex with someone.
54. Sort: south London slang for girlfriend (woman you are having sex with).

is for everything he has done, and I feel his anguish and guilt. I tell him that I will stay, that he should forgive himself and attend Cruse bereavement counselling to come to terms with his loss. I encourage him to hang in there by sharing my own story in the hope that he will be able to see how it's possible to recover from making the wrong decisions, even though you will always mourn the loss of loved ones (Mama for me) and of your baby. I reassure him that we can both learn to live with the constant and ever-present guilt.

OVER THAT WEEKEND, Dave, having unburdened himself of his darkest secrets, becomes more physically demanding. He tells me how much he needs me and how he thinks he's falling in love with me. When I ask him how he knows he loves me, he says it's because he would do anything for me, including a selfless declaration that he would have let me go if I had decided to leave following his confession. We become physically intimate, although it doesn't feel like making love because by his own admission, Dave is not a kisser — he finds it claustrophobic apparently, because he can't breathe properly through a nose that's been broken multiple times over his troubled life.

Not long after New Year's Day, Mary and I can't find Dave anywhere despite scouring all the pubs in Balham, Tooting and Clapham. We're really concerned for his safety because he was suicidally depressed all over Christmas, so I drive towards Streatham after dredging my memory for clues — I recall him mentioning how he used to meet his sort at The Bull in Streatham. I'm disappointed to find him there with her, drunk and no doubt eager to resume where they left off. He's so drunk that it doesn't take much for Mary to persuade him to come home with us. Before she leaves us alone in Dave's flat, she hugs me tight and whispers nervously, "He didn't mean to hurt you, he's just in a lot of pain right now and he isn't thinking straight." We sit in silence for a good ten minutes until the questions I have find a voice.

"Why did you meet with her Dave?"

"I dunno. Just seemed like a good idea at the time."

"What were you planning to do?"

"I dunno. Give her one for the road maybe?" Then, trying to justify when he sees my look of hurt and disbelief, "Come on Simone, it means nothing okay, it's just getting rid of the dirty water! For fuck's sake, it's only a bit of sex!"

I'm seeing all different shades of red now, so I get up and make my way upstairs to the spare bedroom. Dave pushes past me as I get halfway up and blocks my path, grabbing my arm. "Let me go!" I shout. "I can't believe how callous you are, Dave! You say one thing and do another. You've told me how guilty you felt over your affair with her, so I really don't understand how you can hurt me the way you hurt Vicky before she died."

As soon as the words leave my lips, I realise I've said the wrong thing. Dave's eyes blaze brightly, a glacial shade of blue, as if he's retreated behind a thick wall of ice and is no longer present, his pinprick pupils narrowing into black dots of angry aggression. His right fist connects with my left shoulder just above my heart, and the force of the blow is so brutal that I fall backwards and smash my head against the wall at the bottom of the stairs. He follows up with a viciously aimed kick to my ribs, so the air leaves my lungs and I'm unable to speak even if I wanted to. I feel his hands around my neck, squeezing hard in a desperate attempt to stop me from saying anything else. Mercifully, I pass out.

When I come round, I find Dave trying to resuscitate me with the kiss of life, his face wet with tears, eyes back to their normal shade of blue. He tells me how sorry he is as he cradles my head in his lap, how he can't live without me, begging me to never leave him, how he only snapped because I said her name and made him feel guilty, how he just lashed out because he was too drunk and I just happened to be in the way. He starts punching his own chest to demonstrate that he would rather hurt himself than me. He knows I'm a good girl and he doesn't deserve me, but he'll kill himself if I leave him. He's sorry and he'll never do it again. But I have to stop making him do things he doesn't mean to do; I have to stop expecting so much of him because he's just a husk! It's my fault for thinking he's a better man than he is and for showing my disappointment when I realise that he's not.

In a curious role reversal, I find myself hugging and cradling him, soothing away his tears with small kisses, feeling guilty about having triggered his emotional meltdown. I understand how it feels to be in so much pain that you would do anything to avoid thinking about the cause of that pain, drinking yourself into oblivion to numb all sensation, to drown out the accusing voice of Guilt. Drinking so much that you can't think or remember anything. He tries to kiss me, to show love, but it just feels forced and awkward. I reflect on how I've ended up in a relationship with a chor-lang like Pa, and wonder if this is how Mum felt. I conclude that maybe it's because this is all I deserve.

A MONTH LATER on a snowy Saturday morning in February, while Dave has gone for his first plastering job since Vicky's death, I lie propped up in bed still half-drunk from Friday night's shenanigans. I reach out for the bottle of paracetamol on the bedside table and wash down a few tablets with the nearly full litre-bottle of vodka left over from last night. No matter how many pills I take, I can't escape the voracious, gnawingly hungry ache in my chest where Dave punched me, an ache that has grown over time, threatening to consume everything, including me. Oblivion seems like a pleasant destination so I keep going, losing count of how many pills I'm popping, grateful for the empty silence that follows the resounding thud of the bottle when it hits the hard and unyielding parquet floor, before shattering into smithereens.

By some cruel twist of fate, Dave, having got to the job site in North London but returning after an hour and a half to get the favourite trowel he's forgotten, finds me still breathing and calls the ambulance. I'm transported to the hospital and given a stern telling-off by the doctor in A&E about being highly irresponsible and how I'm lucky to be alive. The pills and vodka I consumed are pumped out of my stomach with, surprisingly, no long-term liver damage. The nurses notice the fading bruises around my neck (usually hidden by a scarf for work) and the ones on my chest and ribs. I say I fell down the stairs when they ask why.

Dave drives me home in silence. He waits till we're back indoors before he tells me how angry he is with me for making him miss his first job in months. I need to stop feeling sorry for myself because unlike him, I've had an easy life. He tells me how lucky I am that he loves me, how other blokes would have let a stupid cunt like me die. What was I thinking of, he asks rhetorically. Certainly not him, I'm just being a selfish cunt who drinks so much I forgot how many pills I took. Why can't I think of him for a change? I clearly don't care about how he feels — how he's had to re-live driving to the hospital behind the ambulance carrying Vicky's body. He wishes I were dead instead of her. I'm such a stupid, selfish cunt. I need a good slap so I will wake up and come to my senses. He's got enough to deal with, without having to sort out my shit. He just doesn't need my fucking drama!

"I'm sorry," I reply in a small voice, immediately feeling bad for upsetting him. I'm not even sure if it was a deliberate attempt to kill myself; all I know is, I just wanted the pain to end. A secret part of me wishes that he hadn't found me so I wouldn't be here anymore, until Guilt berates me for only thinking about myself, for not putting his needs before mine. "I'm sorry Dave. I'll try harder, I promise."

"You better or I'll have to give you that slap you deserve!", he shouts over the sound of the front door slamming shut, on his way to the pub for a few pints.

We never speak about this again. I just bury this memory note along with everything else that went before, deep inside my mental stronghold of painful memories. By not speaking of it, we can pretend it never happened. Unspoken words weave thick veils to hide their shards of truth in broken hearts. So, years later, Dave's inability to recollect what he said when he saved my life makes me wonder if it was all just a nightmare, a figment of my overwrought imagination.

Interlude 3

As you join me on my journey, please take a musical break and listen to the song that captures the mood of that particular moment in time. Or read on.

The choice is yours.

"Going Under', *song from the album 'Fallen'
by Evanescence, released August 2003.*

Part Three
Me, UK & New Zealand
(1995 to 2006)

"No one can ever prepare you for what happens when you have a child. When you see the baby in your arms and you know that it's your job now. No one can prepare you for the love and the fear."

Tim Lake, About Time movie 2013, screenplay by Richard Curtis

Chapter 7
Happiness is just a Pipe Dream

LIFE CARRIES ON inexorably — this much I've learnt. Even if you don't want it to. I notice how Dave attracts trouble as a flame draws moths. I find myself planning our move out of London so he can escape the memories and start afresh, after he is convicted for drink driving and loses his licence. I leave for Carterton (we later nickname it Cartoon-town because it is so incongruously new compared to the rest of historic Oxfordshire), three months ahead of Dave, who's tying up loose ends. My new job working for a German IT reseller takes me to Tübingen, a university city that reminds me of Till. I wonder if I made the right decision to end our relationship; I know he would have doted on me even if I didn't deserve his devotion.

One of my colleagues, Joerg, shares my love of Asian culture and history, after a three-year relationship with a Thai girl ten years ago. During my time in Tübingen, Joerg and I grow close (his birthday is only twenty-four days after mine on 26 November). He confides in me about his current relationship issues and hints at wanting more than just friendship. For my birthday in 1995, I receive a delivery at work and am shocked to find, buried underneath a pile of memory boards, a black and red surprise gift box containing expensive-looking luxury lingerie, sized perfectly for me. Cheeks blazing bright red with embarrassment, I hurriedly hide the box in my desk drawer, then send an email to Joerg to thank him and ask how he managed to guess my size. *I can tell just by looking at you,* came the reply, *and I would love for you to show me how well it fits when I visit the UK office in January.* My mind immediately fast forwards to the upcoming weekend and I worry about how Dave will react when I tell him about Joerg's gift. I am honest and loyal to a fault, so I send the gift back to Joerg the same day, along with a handwritten note explaining how sorry I am if I somehow misled him, and how much I value him as a friend, making it abundantly clear that friendship is all I can offer.

The next day, Dave brings me a random bit of privet hedge from London and some chocolates he bought at the train station. I feel touched that he remembered my birthday until he admits it was Mary who gave him a nudge. Not wanting to hurt Dave's feelings, I downplay the monetary value of Joerg's gift, while being truthful about what he wants. "It's made round to go around!" Dave shrugs nonchalantly, "If I don't know about it, it doesn't matter. As long as you don't ever leave me, you can do whatever you want. Actually, you can model it for me and tell him how much I enjoyed the show, especially the extras afterwards!"

Rendered speechless by his crude vulgarity, it takes me a while to process his disturbingly divergent thinking. Later that evening, after he's passed out on the sofa from drinking and I'm gathering clothes for the laundry run, I find in his jacket pocket some girl's name and phone number scribbled in strange handwriting on the distinctive note paper we keep in his London flat. It's way past midnight when he wakes up wanting sex; I refuse his advances, instead asking who she is, my jealous, hurt heart unable to engage further without explanations.

He shrugs again, claiming he can't remember, even when presented with the evidence. I feel betrayed by his apparent inability to reciprocate my loyalty and honesty. His answers sound like excuses and when I threaten to ring the number at a more sociable hour, he becomes agitated and aggressive. Dave told me recently, when we were watching Chelsea thrash West Ham 3-1 after conceding an early goal, that the best form of defence is offence. He demonstrates this tactic now.

"You're completely crazy!" he screams at me, pacing back and forth like a caged tiger. "I promised you I would stop messing around with other girls because it's what you want, even though there's nothing wrong with it. But you keep going on. Vicky was never like you! She loved me no matter what I did. She never criticised me. She just let me do what I want because she trusted me to come home. And I did! I never abandoned her. I would have been there to save her that night if not for my mum's stupid knee operation. We had a great relationship, the best! But now, she's dead and I have to put up with you moaning at me all the fucking time. You need to get over yourself and STOP GIVING ME SHIT! You're a useless cunt, but I can't have my perfect Vicky back however much I want her, so the least you can do is SHUT THE FUCK UP!"

I can see how dangerously close he is to losing it, so I say nothing even though his latest account of events is inconsistent with his original confession. Instead, I pick up the empty beer and wine glasses, making my way into the kitchen with Dave hot on my heels. "Well say something then! We all know you have a smart mouth!" He keeps goading me until I snap,

"Your recollection of what happened with Vicky keeps changing, so I don't know which version to believe. I find it hard to trust you because your actions speak louder than your words. I know I'm broken and flawed. I know Vicky's perfect, but it's really unfair when you compare us because she's already achieved sainthood status and can do no wrong. I can't help it that she's gone, Dave. No one can!"

Without warning, Dave delivers a thumping right uppercut to my nose and follows up with a powerful jab above my right ear. The glasses I'm carrying are propelled from my hands onto the hard and unforgiving tiled floor and fracture into fragments. I feel my nose and ear explode simultaneously with excruciating pain and crumple in slow motion, folding in on myself until the spinning room around me fades into merciful blackness.

IT'S BITTERLY COLD as Dave drives me to the John Radcliffe Hospital. I'm in shock and can only nod as he barks out instructions. My hands are frozen from holding two bags of peas, wrapped in bloody towels, to my nose and temple. This would be funny if it were a movie scene, with the director shouting cut and me wiping away the fake blood. My head feels fuzzy, but I'm alert enough to be alarmed at Dave driving without a licence while over the legal limit. I feel really bad about what happened, how I failed to keep my mouth shut, triggering him into doing what he didn't mean to do.

Dave has already apologised profusely for losing it. He was in tears when I finally regained consciousness after half an hour to find him shaking me so hard, it made my head hurt even more. He didn't mean all the things he said though, he was just lashing out because I was suffocating him with my suspicions. He loves me and needs me, so please, please don't leave, or he would be lost. We have so much to look forward to when he makes the move in January, so let's just get through this, then everything will be right as rain.

I walk into the cold-white, cavernous A&E department on my own, feeling small and ashamed, wishing I were still unconscious or a mute toddler again. Dave's driven home because he wants to avoid the police. It's surprisingly empty at 4am and after multiple X-rays, scans and medication to stop the bleeding and numb the pain, I find myself reciting the words we rehearsed earlier to a couple of kind-looking police officers and triage nurses.

"Well, like I said, I tripped at the top of the stairs and face-planted, while hitting the side of my head on the radiator."

I can see they don't believe me by the looks they're exchanging. One of the officers tries again, sounding very concerned.

"So, your boyfriend is visiting from London and he dropped you off here. Where is he now?" He waits patiently for me to answer.

"He's driven back to Carterton because he could see from my injuries that I would be a while."

"Well, why didn't he come in with you then?" counters one of the nurses.

I explain how traumatic that would be for him because of Vicky and the baby dying so tragically nearly a year ago. "I just had a bit too much to drink and fell down the stairs when I went to get a glass of water. Honestly, I'll be fine once the swelling goes down. See I've stopped bleeding!" They look completely unconvinced but stand aside to make room for the duty doctor who's come to deliver the verdict after reviewing the X-rays and scans.

"By some small miracle, your nose isn't broken although it's going to take a couple of weeks for the swelling to subside. There is a hairline fracture in your skull just above your right temple, but we can't do anything about it except prescribe pain medication. You're concussed from the head injury, and Jane here tells me you've been throwing up, so we're going to have to keep you in until we review you again at 12 noon." Then, softly now as she leans in and places an arm on my shoulder, the compassion in her warm-brown eyes urging me to admit what we all know happened, "Are you sure there isn't anything else you want to tell us, Simone? We're here to help and you deserve to be looked after."

I know I need help. I know Dave needs it too. But I made promises to Mary and Dave, and I can't let them down. I reason with myself — Mum managed to survive Pa's occasional violent outbursts; for decades, they've been able to maintain our 'happy families' image and keep the charade going. They're still together nearly thirty years later. Besides, Dave's not a bad person, he's just depressed and angry about Vicky's death and the loss of their daughter. I shouldn't have said anything, and I shouldn't have questioned or criticised him. Anyway, this is God's way of punishing me for the decisions I made seven years ago; I need to atone for my sins before I'm allowed to be happy. I take a deep breath and exhale, "I'm fine thanks. There's nothing to tell." I look down, as they sigh and walk away.

Eight hours later, the duty doctor with the warm-brown eyes calls after me as I slowly make my way towards the car which Dave has parked right at the far end of the car park to avoid scrutiny. I can tell by his hunched shoulders and frowning face how impatient he is to get going, but she's running towards me now, so I stop and turn around to find her waving some leaflets at me. "Simone, you don't have to say anything but please read these. Take care of yourself. Believe me, it matters. YOU matter." I look down to see leaflets on Relate and Women's Aid, charities known to me during my first job recruiting social workers. I know they help the (usually female) victims of domestic abuse and relationship issues, but I am not a victim. While I appreciate her kindness and thank her sincerely, I don't need any pity or someone to feel sorry for me. I stuff the leaflets in the paper bag holding the pain meds, and get into the driver's seat. I have already let Dave know that I feel well enough to drive because we can't risk him getting into more trouble with the police. He says I've caused enough trouble as it is. We drive home in silence.

I hear Dave casually call up to me when I'm running a bath to wash off the dried blood from my hair, neck and chest. He sounds almost too casual. "Darlin', I'm going to sling this shit (I presume he means the leaflets) in the bin, unless you want them?" I can tell by his tone that he's not asking if he can bin them; he's telling me he's done it and showing me who's in charge. "Yeah sure."

He looms in the now-open doorway, making me jump; I forgot to lock the door. I didn't hear him because my ears are still ringing from earlier. "Here, let me help you." he says, lifting my arms up so he can take my jumper off. I feel suddenly self-conscious about being naked and I just want some privacy, but he's being nice, so I go with it. He stays for a while and watches me wash off the evidence, then squeezes both my shoulders really hard, attempting to massage the tension away. It hurts but I stay silent.

"You know I love you, right?"

I nod once.

"You didn't mention my name, did you?"

I shake my head.

"And you told them you tripped and fell?"

I nod again.

"Good. You're a good girl. I'll leave you to it then. Just shout if you need something."

My head still hurts despite having taken the maximum dosage of pain meds. A small part of me knows I should listen to the duty doctor, get help and leave. But I feel obliged to stay and honour my promises, because Dave needs my help to get better. He's suffered enough loss. I'm sure things will improve once he leaves London for good. Besides, it's too late for me. When Mama was twenty-five, she'd already had six children and was happily married. I've had three failed relationships, four if you count this dysfunctional interaction with Dave. He needs me, he never meant to hurt me. He just lashed out because I made hurtful and insensitive comments when I should have just stayed silent. I promised Mary and Dave I would stay and support them. I feel duty-bound to help him find redemption. Anyway, I'm no angel and I'm still atoning for my past sins. As Mum said all those years ago after my self-inflicted bike accident — I've made my bed, so I'll just have to lie in it. This memory joins its secret sisters in my mental lockbox, never to be spoken of again.

#

IT'S NOT ALL doom and gloom. There are some glimpses of hope when Dave moves up to Carterton permanently, now that he's away from London and the sad memories it invokes. I've been promoted rapidly at work and am earning a decent and stable salary, which is just as well because the income from Dave's cash-in-hand building jobs isn't reliable or regular enough to provide more than fritter money. He's happy that I didn't snitch on him to the police at the hospital, because he's already under caution for a pub skirmish. He's been on his best behaviour since then, because he knows any further transgressions will land him in jail. I still remain mindful of what I say in case I trigger him again. I'm becoming quite the expert at walking on eggshells.

Dave is beginning to enjoy life again after I encourage him to join a nearby village cricket club. He resumes playing the sport he loved as a boy, before life turned him into a thirteen-year-old tearaway who frequented pubs more often than school. After two years of trouble with a capital T, Mary sent him away to a boarding school for badly behaved boys. A single working mum, she just couldn't cope with him anymore. He was eventually expelled for accidentally shooting another boy with an arrow after a late-night archery game went terribly wrong. But Dave seems to be a changed man now. He assures me he never meant for bad things to happen; he just isn't very lucky.

Keen to help him move on, I learn all about cricket and how to score, becoming famous in our local community for my multi-coloured pens, which I use to faithfully record every dot ball and run scored for each batsman facing different bowlers. Each bowler is assigned a different colour, so players can learn about their relative strengths and weaknesses by analysing the coloured patterns. After the first season, I'm asked to join the management committee as Club Fixture Secretary. The logical dreamer in me falls in love with the way cricket is just like a physical game of chess — the perfect blend of brains and brawn that can change the course of a game in just a couple of overs, securing a win through strategic decision-making rather than superior physical prowess. I observe how Dave offers more brawn than brains, although he certainly exhibits a streetwise cunning that I suppose is sometimes more handy than pure academic ability.

The year flies by and just before Christmas, we buy a two bedroom semi-detached cottage in a small rural village within a conservation area, a do-me-up project to tide Dave over the lean winter months, filling in the gaps between jobs. For Christmas, Dave surprises me with a black Labrador puppy, Mungo, who was born on my birthday. We also adopt two cats (brother and sister) from a local animal sanctuary — Whiskey, a tabby, and his sister Ginger, a white and grey who is ginger by nature, not by colour. Life seems sweet. By the summer of 1997, after a fraught period of me handling the planning permission application and mediating between Dave and some of our neighbours who raised objections, the extension is complete and the house has doubled in size. We're sitting on the patio overlooking the rolling Cotswold hills and planning our trip to Thailand, Australia and Singapore, where Dave will meet my parents for the first time.

Recently, Dave has been watching me closely when I interact with some of the cricketers at the club, especially the ones who are single and openly flirtatious. I've never given him any cause for concern but he starts behaving as Adam did with Andrew, questioning my every move and conversation. When he asks why I've been spending more time with Greg (one of younger cricketers from Australia), I jokingly remind him of how he once said it's made round to go around. Instead of laughing, he bristles just the way Adam did. I immediately placate him before his eyes turn glacial blue, saying sorry several times over and explaining that Greg's only been sharing travel recommendations. Crisis averted, we continue planning our holiday until, after dinner, the itinerary is done and dusted.

Out of the blue, Dave casually says, "Well, I suppose we could get married when we're out in Singapore. You know, kill two birds with one stone." I think he's joking, so I laugh it off and start talking about how we'll need to buy insect repellent before we go. "I'm serious Simone. You've been growing on me, a bit like a wart, so we may as well." He fashions a makeshift ring out of the champagne muselet lying on the table and goes to slip it onto my ring finger. I put my hand over his to stop him, lost for words. It's not exactly the most romantic of proposals and he hasn't even got a proper ring. Some would deem this quirky, others quaint. I can't yet work out what I think.

He's always been an impulsively spontaneous person who makes quick decisions on the fly. I'm a ponderer with a tendency to over-think. I tell him I need more time to mull things over, but he presses for a decision, suddenly going all misty-eyed on me. "You're not saying yes because you don't think we'll stay together in the long run. I know you're too good for me, and it's only a matter of time before you find someone else and leave me. I'll be a husk then, with nothing. I've already lost Vicky and the baby. I don't think I could bear losing you too." His tears are free flowing now, as if they've been given permission to fall.

I hesitate, my mind flashing back to our distant and sometimes violent past. He's more Heathcliff than Rochester, we're from totally different backgrounds and I read seven books a week compared to his nil. We don't even like the same music. But I can't deny we've been through a lot together and he saved my life; I've helped him overcome some of his demons, and we both still mourn the loved ones we've lost. He's definitely not my Prince Charming, but sadly, I'm no Snow White either. We're just two wrongs trying to make a right.

"Okay" I say quietly, "Why not." I need to believe that everyone deserves a second chance.

#

Mama passionately believed in portents and premonitions. She experienced this on the day her eldest daughter Marianne died from typhoid. When the Sinseh arrived during a downpour, he entered the room with his black umbrella open, only shutting it once he was inside. Immediately after he left, Marianne deteriorated rapidly, passing away four hours later at exactly 4pm. So much bad luck squeezed into such a short timeframe.

In typical Dave fashion, our itinerary means we are only in Singapore for two days before heading off to Thailand and Australia for two weeks. Dave gives my Mum £100 for one of her solitaire diamond rings which he presents as my engagement ring, and we buy some wedding rings from a Chinatown jeweller in a spare ten minutes before lunch. We leave the rings with my parents for safe keeping, because we plan to backpack through Thailand.

While we're away, I am overcome with a sense of foreboding and I can't shake the feeling that something bad will happen. Dave laughs it off and tells me to stop being so superstitious. Back in Singapore two days before the ceremony, I instinctively ring the boarding kennels to check on our three fur babies, to find that only Ginger survives, both Whiskey and Mungo having crossed rainbow bridge within the first week of us leaving. I am devastated by the loss of my two babies and sob my heart out for the remainder of our time in Singapore. My mental lockbox threatens to explode and unleash its painful contents. I am distraught despite Mum's attempts to console me, and her gentle admonishments that the photos will look like we're attending a funeral instead of a wedding. I'm tempted to postpone, but Dave is determined to go ahead. He remains remarkably dry-eyed, so much so that I worry about him bottling up his grief because I know from my own experience that it's not healthy. Despite my misgivings that somehow this is a message from Mama to call the whole thing off, I marry Dave and we return home to mourn our furry family two days after the wedding. An extremely inauspicious start to our married life, but I remain hopeful that fortune will favour us if we soldier on.

IN THE SUMMER of 1998, I start a new job at Siemens Communications, and become their first female and ethnic Corporate Account Manager in the highly male-dominated world of technology sales. I enjoy helping people innovate to improve their businesses and profits, even though it's a far cry from being a VSO in Africa. I make peace with it by reminding myself that there are multiple ways of helping others, that being financially comfortable isn't necessarily a bad thing, even if it does feel a tad selfish. I am the only female selected for the inaugural Enterprise Leadership Development Programme in addition to my day job, and Dave is so busy with building work we're often like ships passing in the night. I muse about why absence makes the heart grow fonder — perhaps it's because it reduces the friction of time spent together, and therefore, the need to be tolerant of differences.

By June 1999, with time marching relentlessly towards his fortieth birthday in the new millennium, Dave tells me that I'm wedded to my job and broaches the previously taboo subject of having children. I feel the heavy weight of his expectation. This is a big deal for both of us. It's been five years since Dave laid his baby daughter to rest but he feels sure he's moved on. He rarely talks about Vicky now. Twelve years ago, I made the most momentous decision in my life, and it haunts me still. I'm not at all sure that I'm ready to move on. I've always been an all-on or all-off kind of girl. Now I must decide if I really want to open Pandora's box and flick the baby switch to *on*. We spend a month debating the pros and cons, twenty-nine days too long for Dave, nowhere near long enough for me. I love my lists even if Dave doesn't, so I create post-it notes for myself:

Reasons to be childfree	*Reasons to have children*
✗ The world is over-populated	✓ To give/receive unconditional love
✗ Can I keep them safe?	✓ To be a conduit for life and love
✗ Too much responsibility	
✗ Generational baggage	✓ To give them a chance of living
✗ Will I be a good enough mum?	✓ To make a difference
✗ They cost a small fortune	✓ To right the wrongs of the past
✗ Lack of sleep, impact on health	✓ To help and watch them develop
✗ Will we end up like Mum and Pa?	✓ Because my family/hubby/society expects it (Mum keeps hinting!)
✗ Possibility of genetic anomalies	✓ The biological imperative
✗ Little freedom to do as we please	✓ To carry on the family name

Ultimately, I decide it's time to forgive myself for everything that has gone before. I long to feel the movement of a precious tiny person inside me; I long to nurture life and to marvel at its wonder.

On 11 July 1999, I tell my colleagues while they smoke outside our office that I've given up smoking, going from forty a day to zero in the blink of an eye with nothing but sheer will power for support. No nicotine patches, hypnotherapy or acupuncture; just the utmost determination to be the best mum I could ever be. I become a teetotaller, which considering my ten-year-long love affair with substance abuse is a big deal. I had already given up cannabis years ago because of work, but relinquishing alcohol for me is like saying goodbye to your best friend — the emotional crutch who's seen you through thick and thin.

FAST FORWARD ONE and a half years later to December 2000 when we're sitting in the waiting room of the Women's Centre at the John Radcliffe Hospital, waiting to see a consultant about fertility treatment. Dave is agitated, keen to prove his virility, his manliness. I am already preparing myself to accept the blame for our inability to procreate naturally, having endured the laparoscopy procedure and watched the bad news play out on the consultant's face as he discovered the cause of our infertility. It comes as no surprise when we're told that it would be nigh on impossible for me to conceive a baby naturally due to extensive endometrial scarring from the D&C I had years ago. Dave's chest puffs out with pride upon being informed that his sperm count is more than satisfactory, considering he is in his forties after living a life of debauchery. He looks at me pointedly, and we decide to pay for an expensive course of in vitro fertilisation (IVF).

I embark on a soul-destroying cycle of sniffer drugs to downregulate and reset my menstrual cycle to zero, then daily injections to stimulate ovulation, and finally, egg harvesting and fertilisation in a petri dish. We choose two out of the twelve zygotes to be implanted, and leave in hope that Christmas will bring the happy news of being blessed with the pitter-patter of tiny feet the following September. In the coldest of cold nights in January, I go outside to the coal shed to fetch fuel for the fire and feel my womb constrict as though she is expelling all hope. When they confirm at the end of January that the cycle was unsuccessful, I am not surprised, just quietly devastated. "What would you like to do next?" The consultant asks gently. Dave looks at me expectantly, waiting for my answer. "I don't know. Please give me some time and we'll come back to you."

Maybe I'm just not meant to be a mum, not yet. Mama believed the Christian God took eight of her babies to light her path to His one true faith, saving her remaining four children once she renounced paganism. Mum believes that God chooses to bless us with children once we have atoned enough for our sins, that me being barren is His way of punishing me for my past and for straying so far from faith. For the first time in twelve years, I find myself in the confessional at the Holy Trinity Roman Catholic Church in nearby Chipping Norton, asking for absolution in the hope that God will deem me worthy once more.

Interlude 9

As you join me on my journey, please take a musical break and listen to the song that captures the mood of that particular moment in time. Or read on.

The choice is yours.

'More', *song from the album 'Manic' by Halsey, released January 2020*

Chapter 8
Daring to Dream Again

God Forgives Me At Last

I COLLECT THE drugs for the second IVF cycle ahead of our holiday to Chania in Crete for the May bank holiday in 2001. More sniffer drugs and injections for the two weeks that we're away. In the furore of packing while running several major bids at work, I inadvertently leave them behind. Dave is surprised by my unusual distractedness and disorganisation because I always pack everything we need and rarely forget anything. Maybe it's just not meant to be — Mum said as much on our last phone call. "I'm praying for you. Our Lord Jesus will bless you, I'm sure of it, without any medical intervention. Just trust in him and have faith!"

We contemplate asking our only friends in the village to bring the IVF drugs when they join us for the second week of our holiday, but I don't feel comfortable about sharing such private and intimate details. For the first week, I join Dave in drinking the town dry, temporarily relieved from the pressure of staying sober to aid conception. Still hungover on day three, we decide it will be fun to walk the Samaria Gorge. 4km into the 16km hike, I twist my ankle on the uneven, rocky ground. Even though it

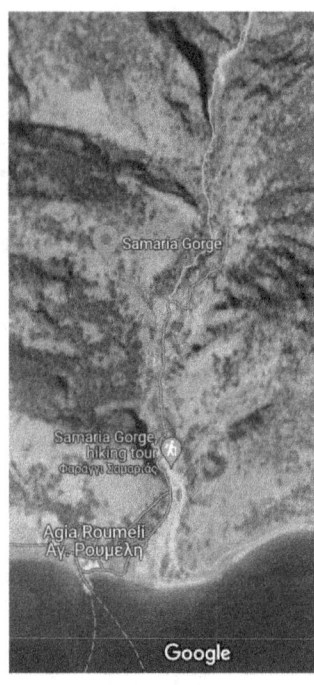

swells up like a balloon, I decide not to bother being airlifted out of the gorge at the halfway checkpoint, convincing the concerned staff that it's just a sprain and not worth troubling anyone for. I grit my teeth and carry on in spite of the bone-crunching pain.

Even Dave is surprised that I manage to complete the trek, especially when the medical team down at the beach end of the trail show me X-rays confirming that I've unknowingly fractured my ankle. I spend the rest of the holiday hobbling around in a cast and boot. By the time John and Becky join us for the second week, I feel like I've drunk enough to last a lifetime and my body stops craving alcohol. Dave teases me about being a bore, but even though I don't know why I no longer fancy drinking, I listen to my body and do as she asks. Three weeks later, I understand why, when the two lines on the pregnancy test herald the dawn of me daring to dream again after fourteen years of wandering in the darkness.

The fertility clinic arranges for an early transvaginal ultrasound scan to ensure I'm not having an ectopic pregnancy due to my (almost) fully blocked fallopian tubes from the endometrial damage I suffered during the D&C. I breathe the biggest sigh of relief when I see the baby's tiny dot-like body resolutely anchored within my uterine walls, and weep when I hear his/her strong heartbeat for the first time. The radiographer, still surprised at the miracle of this natural conception, confirms I'm only about four weeks pregnant, and the clinic staff wish us all the best as they discharge me from their care.

I'M THE HEALTHIEST I've ever been — eating and sleeping well, going for long walks with our rescue dog Kungh (a black lab-collie cross) and Bertie (a tabby cat who behaves like a dog), abstaining from everything except water. I am desperate to ensure the baby has the best start in life. Thankfully, I don't suffer from morning sickness as Mum did, or have any complications at all.

Dave is so busy with work, he has no time to accompany me when I go for ultrasound scans at twelve and twenty weeks. He is noticeably distant after the initial excitement dies down; I can only think this is because he's still struggling to deal with the loss of his daughter from seven years ago, but I decide to let sleeping dogs lie. I choose not to find out the baby's gender, wanting to be surprised, because there are so few pleasant surprises in life as it is. Just as long as he/she is healthy — that's all that matters to me.

In January, my colleagues at Siemens organise a beautiful baby shower where they suggest that the ultrasound image of the baby looks like Alfred Hitchcock, and we laugh and joke about how I will still be typing on my laptop during labour. It's hilarious, but it makes me realise how much my priorities will need to change once this baby arrives.

At the end of January, two weeks before baby's due date on

12 February, I start maternity leave and find myself twiddling my thumbs with nothing to do because the nursery's been ready for two months, and I've already washed and ironed all the baby clothes and bedding several times. Dave seems very much on edge, and says he feels tense because he's not been 'getting rid of the dirty water'.

When we're six days past the baby's due date, the midwife schedules an induction consultation for 21 February. The threat of being induced is enough to shock my body into action because after two hours of constant, intense pain in the very early hours of 19 February, Joe finally decides to make an appearance with a perfect Apgar score[55] of 10. I am completely overwhelmed with feelings so intense, they flood my chest till it feels like I will burst with a myriad of emotions — relief, gratitude, and pure unadulterated love, the kind of love that gives a mother the hysterical strength she needs to lift a car if her child's life depends on it. I stay in the Horton Hospital in Banbury for just one night, most of which I spend staring at Joe while he lies asleep in my arms. As I look out of the window at the starry night sky, I think about the baby I still mourn and realise that the deep hollow inside me, carved from the choices I made as a teenager, allows me now to truly appreciate and hold more joy in my heart, having lived through loss and survived so much sadness.

On his first night at home, Joe sleeps in a Moses basket next to my side of the bed. He wakes up whimpering at around 4am because he needs feeding and I turn on the bedside lamp so I can see to help him latch on. Dave explodes out of bed with an anger so visceral I recoil in shocked surprise. "Do you have to turn on the light? You only ever think about yourself! It's all right for you, I have to work tomorrow."

He slams the room door shut in his rage and I hear other doors slam in succession as he makes his way to the spare bedroom on the other side of the house. I'm too tired to find

---

[55]. Apgar score: test given to new-borns following birth to check **A**ppearance, **P**ulse, **G**rimace response, **A**ctivity and **R**espiration

out why Dave is upset and acting like a big baby, so I wait till Joe has finished feeding before drifting off into a sleepy netherworld filled with dark dreams and unsettling shadows.

While Dave's at work the following day, I find myself full of fear and worry that I am going to be the world's worst mum. All the books I've read about being a new mum describe the warm, fuzzy feelings that accompany your new baby and emphasize the importance of getting the baby to fit into your routine as soon as possible. They recommend letting the baby cry, as it's good for them to exercise their lungs. Not one single book warns you about the panic and fear, the realisation that you are *entirely* responsible for this little person who is 100% dependent on you. It's ridiculous how you have to go on courses and take exams to gain certifications in Excel, project management, how to record cricket scores and to get your driving licence, but no parent gets lessons or needs a licence to give life to and bring up a baby. How utterly ridiculous when it's arguably the single most important job you'll ever have in your life! Are we just meant to muddle through?

I move my L-shaped nursing pillow and Joe's Moses basket into the spare bedroom before Dave comes home. He doesn't appear to notice. The explosive anger of last night has simmered down to a sullen sulkiness which I haven't got the time or patience to deal with. By the weekend, I find it's easier just to co-sleep with Joe in the double bed, and the Moses basket gets relegated to the nursery where we only go for bath time or to look at the Winnie-the-Pooh wall stencils. Joe is a very content and placid baby in general, but he turns into an unhappy, windy whinge-bag at night when my supply of breast milk has slowed and we're both running low on energy and patience.

On the fifth night, Dave loses it while Joe is grizzling and utters the most hurtful words I've ever heard: "I wish you were both dead instead of Vicky and my daughter." I catch a glimpse of those frighteningly familiar glacial blue eyes and retreat to the spare bedroom, choking back tears and the angry retorts that I know will only rile him into physical frenzy, earning me another anguished trip to A&E. Some things are better left unsaid.

I REMEMBER READING about how the best-laid plans of mice and men often go awry, which I'm sure was paraphrased from 'To a Mouse' by Robert Burns. I had planned to return to work after six months, expressing enough milk, supplemented by formula, to leave Joe in Dave's care during the day. We are living off the sales commission I'd saved up over the seven years since 1995, so things are financially comfortable for now, although not sustainably so in the long run. The first time I try to wean Joe onto a bottle of cows' milk formula, he refuses to drink, and there ensues six solid hours of frustrated crying until he is so hungry he drinks the whole bottle in five minutes. I'm an emotional wreck by now, full of guilt for denying my baby what he needs, both breast pads soaked through with breast milk from my body's instinctual response to Joe's hungry cries.

Joe has fallen asleep from the entirely exhausting experience. I go to lay him down in his basket when he jolts awake like a child possessed and projectile vomits all over me onto the wall. His skin has turned a nasty, blotchy shade of vermillion with angry-red raised welts spreading rapidly over his face and body. Alarmed, I wrap him up in a blanket, stick him in his car seat and drive like the wind, breaking all speed limits, to our local GP's surgery. They can see how frantic I am with worry, covered in vomit and smelling of rancid formula, but thankfully, they remain calm and reassuring. The doctor informs me that Joe appears to have had a severe allergic reaction to the formula. She attempts to inject him with antihistamine but listening to my maternal instincts, I refuse to let her and hold him to my breast instead. Within ten minutes, Joe's skin returns to normal and he snuffles in his sleep contentedly, finally satisfied after the ordeal I've subjected him to. I carry on breastfeeding him for as long as he needs.

Seven months later in September 2002, I hand in my notice at Siemens, explaining to my boss Andy, who has young children too, that my son comes first.

Since Joe's allergic reaction, Dave and I have been discussing plan B. I've been ignoring the signs of his disintegration for a while now, hoping against hope that he will turn things around, but he's fallen out spectacularly with almost all of our neighbours including John and Becky, over the most innocuous things — a disagreement over the weather, where and how he parks his car, them not saying hello or saying it in that tone he doesn't like. Now that I'm not there to mediate, Dave has run riot and reacted without thinking about potential consequences. I receive call after call from concerned friends at the cricket club, asking if Dave is all right because he is so moodily angry nowadays. I resigned from my role as Club Fixture Secretary a couple of months before Joe's arrival and haven't been able to accompany Dave to matches at the weekend, especially because Joe needs my full and undivided attention.

The final straw comes when our nearest neighbour, the farm owner whose female dog Kungh has impregnated with unwanted puppies, threatens to call the police after an altercation with Dave over unmended fences turns ugly. I try to placate everyone, but Dave thinks it is time for us to move on to pastures new. Too many bridges have been burned; it's all beyond mending. It feels very much like the great escape from London eight years ago.

For a while now, Dave's had his sights set on New Zealand, so while Joe is napping, I am tasked with investigating and applying for residence permits, as well as planning a trip in January 2003 to scout for jobs and a place to live. We visit Singapore in December 2002 enroute to New Zealand. Mum sees the tension between Dave and me, and utters the same words Mama said to her thirty-seven years ago, *Mone, yee si chor-lang*[56]. I don't want to admit what we both know to be true, so I say nothing, as tears of resignation fill my eyes and spill unbidden onto the unyieldingly

---

56. Yee si chor-lang: Hokkien for "He is an uncouth ruffian".

cold marble floor of my parents' posh District 10 condo. I've made my bed, so I'll just have to lie in it.

Twice Blessed

WE'RE GOING TO be hazelnut farmers. At least, that's the plan. Buoyed by the favourable exchange rate and the potential of reaping three NZ dollars for every British pound, Dave is gung-ho about our new life in New Zealand. I try to muster the same level of enthusiasm, but fall short when I realise it's me who has to be the main breadwinner for our family until the farms are planted and established, me who has to leave Joe in Dave's care while desperately expressing milk late at night to ensure he gets the sustenance he needs. It breaks my heart to leave Joe when I start a new job as International Sales Manager for CES Communications sixteen months after he's born, but I know I have to — needs must when the devil drives. Dave jokes about how he'll finally have to change a nappy for the first time, now that I'm 'The Wallet'. We've brought Kungh with us and I feel so guilty that we've left Ginger and Bertie behind with Mary. I've abandoned two-thirds of my furry family, leaving my loved ones behind, but I don't have time to dwell on regrets. Onwards and upwards, as Dave always says.

While waiting for our UK house sale to finalise, the UK's economic growth plummets spectacularly and Dave becomes morosely angry about how the tides have turned. Every pound will now only fetch about 1.8 dollars. We have bought two adjacent plots of land but have to live in limbo till the exchange rate improves before building our dream house in Amberley, 46km north of Christchurch in South Island. We're living in a palatial four-bedroom rental in posh Fernside, rattling around inside its four walls, the house full up to its rafters with Dave's discontent. I go to work every day desperate to return home so I can nurse Joe and hug him, while keeping a watchful eye on Dave and his rapidly unravelling emotions.

Things come to a head in June 2003 when Dave greets me at the door after I get home from work to explain how he's grabbed our landlord by the throat, all because he had the temerity to mow the lawns on the ride-on without notifying us beforehand. I don't have much time to react, and watch in disbelief as Dave punches himself on his left arm creating self-inflicted bruises and red punch marks on his skin.

Ten minutes later, our doorbell rings and I open the front door to find two policemen asking to speak to Dave. I manage to mediate while Dave shows them his self-inflicted injuries which he blames on our landlord, effing and blinding throughout the exchange. I scoop Joe up when he toddles round to peek shyly at the policemen who smile at him and play peekaboo until he giggles. Joe's laugh diffuses the palpable tension. I can see how they don't want to take this further and am grateful when they leave, after issuing a caution for Dave to be on his best behaviour. Apparently our landlord doesn't wish to press charges anyway, so I make a mental note to call and thank him. As soon as their squad car disappears down the driveway, I take Joe out of the house pretending I need something from New World in Rangiora, so he doesn't have to listen to Dave ranting on and on about the 'fucking pigs'. The last thing I want is for Joe to develop an aversion to the kind people who are just doing their best to protect us and to keep the peace.

Not long after, even though Dave and I are hardly ever intimate because we've not shared the same bed since Joe was born, and while I am on the mini-pill because I'm still breastfeeding, I find out I am pregnant again. I feel conflicted because work is so busy and we've just launched our Australian subsidiary — the timing totally sucks, but is there ever a good time to have a baby? I feel immense wonder and gratitude for being blessed by God again, so I embrace this gift of a child with hope and excitement.

Dave is ambivalent about this unplanned pregnancy. I know how relieved he was when Joe turned out to be a boy, because he was dreading a daughter who would remind him of his loss. He is not at all interested in attending any of the ultrasound scans — at six weeks to check if the pregnancy is ectopic, at twelve weeks to monitor for warning signs of genetic anomalies, or at the twenty-week developmental scan. I am alone on this journey, but happier that way. When I see my little bean flipping around on the screen and hear their steady heartbeat, I can't wait till the bean is big enough for me to feel that intimately unique bond formed when nurturing a child inside me.

I know that Dave needs a new environment to help him recover normality, so we buy another do-me-upper in Rangiora, which is only half an hour from Christchurch, and move away from Fernside to avoid further aggravation. The move sucks up the last of my savings and increases the pressure on me to bring home the bacon. The only things that keep me going are Joe and my unborn Beanie. I love my babies wholeheartedly with the most fervent wish for their happiness. I would do anything to ensure they stay happy, that they always feel safe and loved.

Dave does his best to derail our life — he falls out with our new next-door neighbours Craig and Angela (all because her annoying and irritating voice grates on his nerves), and the family across the road for just being there. He tells me how much he hates living cheek by jowl with other people. He is constantly frustrated by the delay on our house-building plans and the declining exchange rate.

During one of his alcohol-induced confessions, he reveals how he's felt irritated for years, particularly by women. How he would have to leave his mum, nan and even Vicky after a short while of being in the same room, because their voices would grate on his nerves until he felt like hitting them to shut them up. He divulges the dirty little secret desire he used to harbour when people-watching out of his flat window in London — how he would imagine dragging a female jogger into his flat, raping her while choking her with his bare hands, then disposing of her body across the common on the railway tracks during the cover of darkness. He admits the only thing that stopped him was the fear of being caught and losing his freedom. He tells me how his mum made him sleep in the lounge after she caught him looking up his sister's nighty at her 'bits' when he was six. He assures me he's a reformed man, that all these dark desires stopped as soon as I saved him by removing him from the bad influences in London. That I am the only one who will listen to him without judging or criticising, the only one he trusts to keep his dark thoughts secret.

I begin to look at him in a disturbing new light — I wonder whether we can ever truly trust anyone or really know them. Mama always taught me that there is good and bad in everyone, that there is no such thing as a bad person, just misguided souls who sometimes make bad choices. So I focus on the good part of Dave's confession — ultimately, he chose to rise above his base desires and walked away from the urge to do seriously bad deeds. Even so, I despair at the thought that our life will never ever be normal again without my (or some divine) intervention.

Meanwhile, my little Beanie grows inside me and I feel their soul through their many subtle movements in my womb. Beanie is particularly active during the early hours of the morning, a night-owl just like me. The strangest thing happens while I am three months pregnant — Joe is now able to fall asleep without me, and every time I go past his room, I hear him chatting animatedly to an unknown being. One night when curiosity gets the better of me, I open the door and ask him who he is talking to. His answer doesn't surprise me — "I'm talking to a lady who looks just like you Mummy, but her hair is white and she's dressed funny. Her hair is all up at the back of her head, like this…"

He scrunches up his tiny hand to make a bun-shape. Mama is talking to her great grandson. I still miss her so much.

Four months into my pregnancy, my midwife and a consultant gynaecologist summon me for a crisis meeting:

"You're poisoning your baby."

"Oh my God! How so?"

"Well, your blood proteins are incompatible — your big C vs their little c and your little e vs their big E."

"So, what does this mean?" I ask, completely distraught and panicking about how I'm harming Beanie.

"It means you'll have to undergo fortnightly blood tests to check if the antibodies you're producing are nearing levels toxic enough to damage the baby's liver, which can lead to organ failure and possibly even death!".

I can absolutely do blood tests. In fact, I would give all of the blood in my entire body to ensure Beanie's survival. I endure fortnightly tests to monitor the antibody levels, my arms soon resembling those of a long-term drug addict. It's touch and go, but the levels slowly rise over the remaining five months. The doctors are on standby to extract Beanie via C-section should the antibody levels rise beyond the crisis threshold.

Two months before Beanie's due date of 4 May, Joe stops breastfeeding and tells me, "I'm all growed up now Mummy, baby needs milk more than 'oe."

He still loves to cuddle close though. I chuckle at how he still struggles to pronounce his J's. I accept his growing independence, love his selflessness, and focus instead on the little life who will soon join us. Joe is extremely excited about his new sibling and helps me prepare the nursery. We read stories like 'There's A House Inside My Mummy' over and over, and he spends all of our cuddle time with his arms wrapped around my growing belly, talking to Beanie about how they will soon be playing his favourite game of hide and seek, rather than Mummy, who is very bad at hiding.

As soon as I get home from work and during weekends, Dave is straight out of the door, glad to be relieved of his daddy day care duties. I'm happy with our 'ships-that-pass-in-the-night' arrangement because I can see he needs the breathing space, plus it saves me having to practice my eggshell-walking skills.

He spends most of his time with Ian, father to Emily, Joe's best friend from pre-school. Since we've moved to Rangiora, Dave has alienated everyone except Ian and his family; he warns me against getting too close to people at work or telling them too much about our lives. The suspicious and cynical Londoner from ten years ago is always lurking — 'You can take the boy out of London but you can't take London out of the boy!'. He's particularly proud of this phrase, often used by one of our friends at the cricket club in Oxfordshire, friends we left behind when we moved country.

At 3.30am on Tuesday, 20 April, exactly two weeks before Beanie's actual due date, I wake up in agony. I immediately shake Dave awake and page our midwife Lynda, who calls back twenty minutes later, urging us to get to Rangiora Hospital as soon as we can. Ian turns up thirty minutes later to stay with Joe, who is still sleeping. Dave drives me there like a madman, nearly running over some of the sheep which have wandered from the open fields on either side of the hospital driveway. He swears profusely,

"Fucking sheep, for fuck's sake, whose idea was it to move out here? It's the bloody back of beyond!"

I nearly laugh out loud with the ironic retort stuck in my head — *I think you need to look in the mirror*, but I'm in too much pain to do anything except breathe. Lynda has to drive at least forty-five minutes from the other side of Christchurch to get to us, so by the time we get to the hospital, it's the duty midwife who steps in. It's ten minutes to five and we make our way slowly up the interminably long corridor, no time to get a wheelchair. After I've climbed onto the bed facing away from the midwife on my knees, she attempts to position the pinard so she can listen to the baby's heartbeat. I wave her away impatiently, explaining in short sharp pants that I need to push, there's no time because ready or not, Beanie's coming right now! My waters break soon after and with two firm pushes, Beanie is born at exactly 5.02am, settling quickly on my chest after a few cries announce her arrival. One look into her beautiful midnight-blue eyes is all it takes for me to recognise her old soul, and to fall in love with her all over again.

By now, Lynda is here. Aware of my medical history and the need to deliver all of the placenta, she hands Beanie over to Dave, asking him to hold his new-born daughter. I hear him respond in a deeply disappointed voice, "Oh, it's a girl." My heart sinks, suddenly aware that despite his assurances about having moved on, he is still stuck in the bitter winter of 1994, still angry at how life has robbed him of happiness, allowing his past to cloud his present. I file this realisation away in my mental stronghold of unspoken thoughts because I am too preoccupied with what the paediatrician is saying after he checks Beanie over.

"Apgar score of 9 Simone, because she's slightly jaundiced from the antibodies. But we'll get her under the UV lamp right away and she'll soon turn a perfect shade of pink, don't you worry. I'll just grab some blood to check the exact levels."

But Lynda can see how concerned I still am, so she tries to distract me by asking what name we've decided on.

"Samaria" I reply, unable to take my eyes off her now she is back at my breast, nestled snugly within the cradle of my arms. Named after the Samaria Gorge, where I first began this journey to have my children; and because I've been travelling down a long and rocky road, enduring much pain and sadness, to hold her once more.

DAVE LEAVES BEFORE they wheel us into our room, keen to get home so Ian can go to work. Lynda helps me to unpack my overnight bag, which includes a present from Beanie to Joe, so he will feel he is gaining love rather than losing attention. There is no need to worry though, even though the first scene he walks in on, is a big no-no in all the 'how to prevent sibling rivalry' books. Breastfeeding on demand means that I am unable to stage-manage what Joe sees when he walks in. He runs straight past his present, making a beeline for the sofa where I am feeding his sister, a big smile

spreading across his cheeky little face as he chatters excitedly, "Let's play hide 'n' seek now, baby."

Chapter 9
Muted

'Oe do it Mummy, let 'Oe do it! For the last two weeks, my little helper has been laying out the cushioned mat and watching closely while I carry Samaria to and from the large window sill in our open plan living area for her daily dose of UV. Our little princess still needs the sun to banish the last vestiges of toxic antibodies circulating in her bloodstream. She is thriving and growing well.

Although I still worry about whether I will be a good mum to Beanie, I feel better able to cope with the incessant wind-induced night time crying. I avoid eating food Joe is allergic to, so I don't pass on the same sensitivities and intolerances to Samaria through

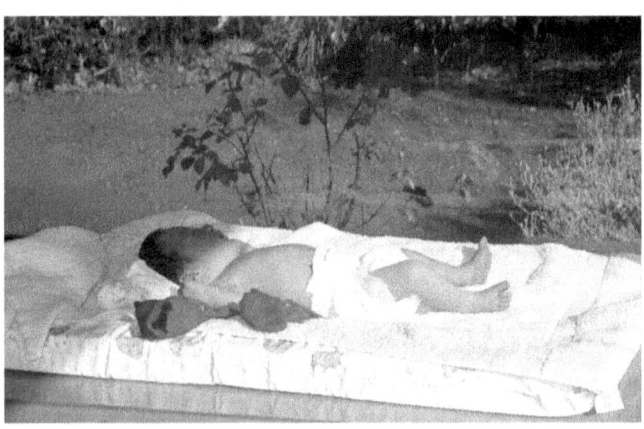

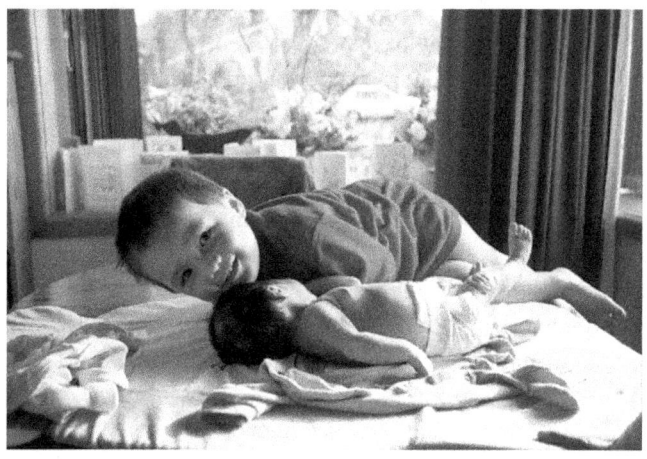

my breast milk. I'm just muddling through this mum business with only my babies' cries and voices to guide me. Books don't help here — too theoretical. It takes twice as long to do anything with an excited toddler getting under your feet, but I love how Joe is being the caring big brother I always hoped he would be. I enjoy watching him learn how to change nappies and cuddling Samaria to sleep on the sofa. I'm sure he would breastfeed her himself if he could.

Dave has been vacillating between being a doting Dad and a mercurially moody stranger who snaps like a great white shark every time Joe tries to help or we get under his feet. We no longer have the spacious safety net of absence with me being on maternity leave; instead, being so physically close is breeding a claustrophobic climate of contempt. I sense his increasing levels of irritation and try my best to lower the tone of my voice so it is less shrill and strident. Recently, Dave has been telling me to *take it down a level Simone!*, dropping his hand, palm facing downwards, from up near his face down to his hips, while making a humming sound that starts off loud and high, dwindling down to a soft, low and barely audible whisper.

HM
MM
Mm
mm
mm
mm
mmm

Remembering what Dave said about how he sometimes hates women's voices, I acquiesce and try my best to be less loud, anxious to keep the peace, to avoid the glacial blue iciness of his rage. I'm permanently on tenterhooks, living so close to the edge I feel like life will soon slide off the precipice and crash onto the ragged rocks below; the veneer of normality smashing open to reveal the reality of living with the poor choices I've made so far. I'm trying desperately to hold things together for my two-year old toddler and two-week old baby, who mean the whole world to me. The hurricane is on its way, and try as I might, I know I won't be able to stop it.

The storm breaks in the most innocuous way you can imagine. Samaria is asleep in the lounge area safely strapped into her car seat, Joe is watching his favourite Teletubby Po help Noo Noo clean up some spilled custard, and Dave is chopping up organic carrots to make a stew in the kitchen area around the corner. I've just finished tidying up when Joe asks if I can refill his Tommee Tippee cup with apple juice. As soon as I open the fridge door, I sense Dave's simmering anger is close to boiling point. He snarls through bared teeth,

"Do you have to do that now? Can't you see I'm busy? There's no space!"

I try to placate him. "Dave, I'm just trying to refill Joe's juice, it won't take a minute and I'll be out of your hair soon."

"You're always getting under my feet and getting in the way. Why do I have to do everything around here? You're fucking useless and lazy! You should be cooking, not me. What's your excuse, you're not working at the moment!"

I close the fridge door and back off with the juice carton towards the dining area, meaning to refill Joe's cup without responding, but the dam of words I've been holding back for years breaches under the pressure of postpartum hormones, plus a rebellious urge to speak up against his unjust and unfounded criticism. I hear my louder-than-usual voice retort sarcastically,

"In case you haven't noticed, it's a full-time job moving

country, being the main breadwinner and looking after three babies. You need to grow up!"

I look down to see Joe standing next to me, hopping impatiently from foot to foot, about to start whining for his drink. I refill his cup, ignoring the daggers I can feel from Dave's now murderously glaring eyes and put the juice carton back in the fridge.

"There you go with your fucking smart mouth! You've always got to have the last fucking word, haven't you? I don't even know why I put up with you. You're a crap fuck, you're fat, you're a shit wife and a bad mum. Who would want to be married to you? Not me. If the exchange rate were better, I'd be off, away from you and your fucking strident, loud voice! I FUCKING HATE YOU, YOU USELESS LAZY CUNT!"

Fear is screaming at me to walk away for the sake of the children, to avoid the inevitable showdown, but Fairness is bristling for a fight, demanding for her voice to finally be heard. I walk a few steps into the kitchen area, away from the dining and living areas, trying to keep the commotion contained, away from the children. Fairness wins, even though Fear cautions that there will be no winners here unless someone backs down. Fairness speaks up in a calm and quietly querulous voice,

"If you hate me so much, then just leave. We can get divorced and I'll go back to Singapore and live with my parents until I work out what to do next. You're clearly unhappy, so let's just call it a day while we can."

Stunned by my response, Dave stops chopping, knife suspended in mid-air as if we're stuck in a time warp and we've gone back to ten years ago, when he first pushed me down the stairs before kicking and choking me into unconsciousness.

"You bitch! You selfish bitch! You've sucked all the life and money out of me until I'm a husk, you've turned me into a housewife doing women's work and looking after the children so you can have a career. And now you've got your two precious brats, you're just going to walk away?"

"They're your children too, Dave! I would be more than happy to stay at home bringing up Joe and Beanie, but we've been over this so many times! I have to work because it's the only way we'll earn enough for the lifestyle you want. I'm sorry, but I just can't do this anymore!"

With that, I turn away from him and open the door to the hallway, stepping through and going to close it, just as he shouts out "DON'T YOU FUCKING DARE! DON'T YOU DARE WALK AWAY FROM ME, YOU FUCKING BITCH!". His pin-prick pupils narrow into steely daggers aimed dangerously at my head, followed soon after by his hand. I watch in horror, as if events are unfolding in slow motion, as the Global steel knife flashes like a blurrily spinning stream of silver towards my face. Adrenaline kicks in and I pull the door towards me in a purely reflexive reaction, just in time for the knife to land and embed in the wooden door where my head was a few micro-seconds ago. Fear takes over and I scream desperately at him to "GET OUT! Just get out!"

He lunges for me, eyes glazed over like he's possessed by the devil himself, pushing me backwards onto the carpeted hallway floor, his builder's hands closing around my throat and squeezing so hard, it's as if he wants to wring the life out of me. I start to pass out but fearing for Joe and Beanie, I try to fight him off, loosening his grip just enough to croak out "Stop Dave, please stop. The children. Please stop."

He doesn't register what I say, my voice too soft to reach him, but he hears the piercing distress call coming from little Joe, who's watching this horror movie play out before him. He wails loudly while trying to pull his dad off me,

"Stop it Dad! You're hurting Mummy!"

My heart breaks at our two-year old son trying so hard to be the man his father isn't. I hear the back door slam seconds later while holding my boy close and comforting him as best as I can, choking back my own sobs so he can cry his heart out. The only saving grace about this sorry situation is Samaria sleeping soundly through World War III.

I AM VERY calm, very subdued, like all the stuffing has been knocked out of me as I autopilot my way through the rest of the afternoon and evening. I finish off the stew after prising the knife from the door. Two hours later, Joe thanks me for his "deelishoes dins dins", his large, long-lashed eyes happy again now that peace has resumed. Samaria feeds contentedly while cradled in my arms and I have them both bathed, smelling sweetly of talcum powder and innocence, tucked up in bed by 7pm after reading 'Goodnight Moon' three times.

I spend the next few hours staring at the night sky, wondering if I should call my parents now and explain how I need to come home with my tail between my legs, but I know they have their hands full with Steph, who they still support financially because her bipolar disorder prevents her from working. More than anything though, I'm afraid to admit failure, to leave the bed I've made through my poor choice of staying with Dave in spite of our rocky start, all because I believed he deserved a second chance. I know most marriages need to be worked at and fairy tale endings are more often the result of compromise and tolerance, rather than those unrealistic dreams I used to

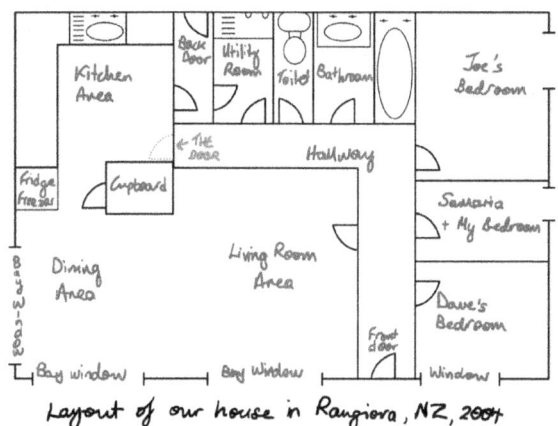

Layout of our house in Rangiora, NZ, 2004

have of finding true love with my Prince Charming. But I never imagined I would end up with a man like Heathcliff; up till now, I preferred to think that Dave was more like Rochester — flawed but worthy of redemption.

Dave stumbles through the kitchen and into the living room area just after midnight while I am feeding Samaria, reeking of alcohol and regret.

"I'm sorry. I shouldn't have lost my temper like that. I would never knowingly hurt you (*I hear myself think — but you threw a knife at me!*) You know I've been so stressed about the exchange rate and impatient to start building our dream home (*Don't I just?*) I just want to get the hazelnut farm going soon, so you can stay home and look after the kids. (*If only! Mum was right when she said don't depend on a man.*) You three are the only good things that have ever happened to me! I love you all so much, and can't bear the thought of you leaving me. I'll do anything to make you stay (*You said that last time*) Please stay, Simone. You promised you'd never leave me (*But why don't you keep your promises?*) Please stay so the kids will grow up with their daddy. I never had a dad and look at what happened to me. I'm just a husk. I'm nothing without you."

He's crying now, full on weeping while holding on to us tightly, as if his life depends on it. I feel so much sympathy for him, it's as if his tears have extinguished the dying embers of angry indignation in my heart. Fear tries to speak — what if he does this again? Empathy reminds me that it's been nine years since he last lost it, and I was sarcastic when I didn't need to be. I should have left those harsh and critical words unsaid.

Samaria has finished feeding so I support her head on my shoulder while gently rubbing her back to bring up trapped wind. Dave's still holding on for dear life. He begs fervently, sincerely,

"Please say you'll stay. Please."

He gets down on his knees in front of us.

"Please?"

After a long internal struggle, I nod yes. I feel meekly muted and emotionally overwhelmed, unable to trust my voice to say anything.

Interlude 5

As you join me on my journey, please take a musical break and listen to the song that captures the mood of that particular moment in time. Or read on.

The choice is yours.

'Nobody Knows', *song from the album 'I'm Not Dead'*
by P!nk, released November 2006

Part Four
Me, UK
(2006 to 2022)

"Hope is a good thing, maybe the best of things, and no good thing ever dies."

Andy Dufresne, 'The Shawshank Redemption' movie 1994, based on the novella Rita Hayworth and Shawshank Redemption by Stephen King

如果没有黑暗, 星星就不会发光
(rú guǒ méi yǒu hēi àn, xīng xīng jiù bù huì fā guāng)
If there is no darkness, stars cannot shine.

Chinese proverb, author and date unknown

Chapter 10
Time to Move On

THE GBP TO NZD exchange rate languishes in the doldrums for two years, along with Dave's dashed dreams. We live in a permanent state of tension, temporarily relieved when Mum and Pa visit us for Christmas 2005, staying till early 2006 to spend time with their grandchildren. I take some time off to look after the children so Dave can show Pa around Christchurch. Despite having spent three Christmases in the height of New Zealand's sweltering summer, Dave still misses the traditional British roast dinner with all the trimmings.

We religiously follow government guidance to protect Joe and Samaria from harmful UV rays, but they soon develop sun spots and freckles. The only thing Dave enjoys about living in New Zealand is his permanent suntan, although he raises concerns about the sun's damaging impact on the kids, and recruits my parents to join him in his campaign to persuade me that we should move back to the UK. I don't need much persuading, especially when a Kiwi friend of mine becomes the unlucky one in twenty people who develops skin cancer in New Zealand. She is back at work a week after the operation as though she's had a tooth removed, rather than a tumour.

#

I FLY BACK to the UK in March 2006 and stay with Robin, a good friend from my Siemens days, for two weeks, leaving Dave with bags of expressed breast milk for Beanie. I find a job at APD Communications after attending several interviews, while co-ordinating the New Zealand house and land sale, plus organising international removal quotes and sorting out UK pre-schools for the children. Dave has always left everything for me to organise; before I came along, Mary did everything for him so she couldn't wait to abdicate the role and responsibility to me.

In April 2006, just after Samaria's second birthday, three years after we first emigrated to New Zealand in search of the promised land, I find myself staying at Robin's during the week to be closer to work and making the most of weekends with the children at Mary's house in Oxfordshire. Dave is very particular about choosing a new house, so we find ourselves going further north and west to get the perfect property. Finally we choose a house set in one and a half acres of land with a five-hundred-year-old oak tree marking its north-east boundary. It's near the quaint market town of Tenbury Wells, which does not have a single High Street branded shop, only independent boutique shops, artisan cafés which make their own ketchup, and a family-run, farm-based supermarket called Bowketts.

When we eventually move into our new home in late summer, we get to know one of neighbouring families well, because Val and Gary have a daughter who is only twenty-one days older than Joe. We're in a three-house enclave, in the middle of rural Worcestershire, set about two miles off the Tenbury-to-Bromyard road, down a steep incline onto a winding shared drive which eventually branches off into three separate driveways.

Dave ignores one of the families (elderly with grown-up children) because he thinks they are obstructive snobs after they object to our application for planning permission to extend the house and build a detached indoor swimming pool room and sauna. Dave says he won't be happy till he's finished building the dream house he wanted in New Zealand, so I mediate once more with all involved parties to help him find his happy. I just long for a peaceful life, and am able to find joy living anywhere the children are; their laughter lights up my life and lifts my spirits.

Once again, I become the main breadwinner while Dave is the house husband who takes on ad hoc building jobs when the children are at school or nursery. My work selling mobile communications and control room solutions to public sector organisations takes me all over the UK from Cornwall to Glasgow, although I mainly spend time in our Hull head office or Milton Keynes sales and marketing base. I become close to our Legal Director, Hilary who is married with two daughters, because she is acerbically witty, full of good advice and a loyal friend. My life is full of friendships with strong women. I still keep in touch with Mave, who is now a high-flying legal eagle in Singapore, Bridget who re-trained to become a human rights lawyer in London juggling work with being mum to IVF twins, uni friends Jen, Deli and Sarah, and Kiwi work buddies Lesley and Rachel.

Since I always regulate what and how much I say during conversations with Dave, work is one of the few places I can actually use my voice and be heard, so I relish meeting my new colleagues, introducing myself and learning about them. It's during one of these illuminating intros that I meet Doug, Quality

General Manager responsible for compliance and business-critical certifications, at our Milton Keynes office on 10 August 2006. Doug is sitting quietly minding his own business at one of several hot desks when I bustle into the room and make a beeline for the vacant desk opposite. I ask politely if I can sit there, introduce myself enthusiastically and start quizzing him, curious to learn more about the person behind those gold-tinged grey-green-blueish eyes framed behind metal-rimmed glasses. His equally curious eyes draw me in, inviting me to bare my soul, unlocking a strong sense of déjà vu, taking me back centuries to the halcyon days of King Arthur and the Knights of the Round Table, making me feel like a damsel in distress who is in desperate need of being rescued. We feel instantly connected and understood. We discover a shared love of Goth, New Romantic, Punk and Eighties' music during our thirty-minute conversation. Which I'm sure he feels is more like an interrogation as I probe into how and what he really thinks about business management, the psychology of persuasion, how to do the right things and do them well. I see in his expressive eyes the boy who dreams of making a difference hiding behind a cynical cloak of lived experiences, and conclude, "You know Doug, for someone who is all about compliance, you're a real non-conformist and very Machiavellian, but in a good way of course!"

We both laugh out loud, completely at ease with each other, having shared more in thirty minutes than most people do in a lifetime. The logical dreamer in me whispers wistfully, *Where have you been all my life? You're like an oasis in the desert! I've been searching for you all this time.*

HILS AND DOUG become my closest friends and for the first time in my life, I start to confide in them about my tempestuous relationship with Dave, sharing my concerns that Joe and Samaria are being adversely affected. I am away most of the week with work, and start to receive calls from Joe when he wakes up to find that Dad has left them on their own in the dark house. When I finally track Dave down, he explains he only popped out for one drink and promises not to do it again; a promise he struggles to keep.

One weekend, Joe confesses to feeling conflicted. He's been experiencing issues with another boy at school, a troubled soul who found his mum's body hanging lifeless after she sadly sought solace in suicide, while his dad was behind bars for beating his mum up. I watch Joe's worried face as he explains how Dad said to 'take the bully round the back of the bike shed and punch him. Oh and don't tell your mum I said so!' I ask Joe what he thinks is the right thing to do and his reply reassures me: "I don't want to punch him Mummy. He seems really sad, and I want to be kind like you always say to be. Anyway, my teacher knows and she stops him from hurting us."

I hug him close and praise him for making the right choice. I'm deeply dismayed about Dave undermining me as a parent, with his underhanded, uncompassionate and petulantly childish advice. When I ask Dave what led to Joe's conflict and explain how we need to present a united parental front despite our different perspectives, he becomes defensive but manages, just, to control his temper. I overhear him saying to Mary on the phone later that he's trying to keep the peace, jokingly ending the conversation with, "Well, got to dash Mum, go cook dinner, get the pinny on and do women's work. I've got to keep Simone happy because we wouldn't want The Wallet walking away now, would we?"

I know it's a joke but as Mama always said, many a true word said in jest.

#

IN FEBRUARY 2007, Dave becomes restless with impatience while we wait for approval from the council planning officer, without which he cannot commence building work on the house extension. To brighten up his mood and diffuse the tension, I pay for a week's holiday in the Algarve for Dave and the children. I'm shocked when I receive a collect call from Dave interrupting my meeting, asking if I can wire some money across because he forgot his bank card. When I ring him back a few hours later with details of how to access the wire transfer, his irritated comment beggars belief — "Hang on! I can't write that down because you didn't pack a pen!" I wait for ten minutes while he goes down to the hotel reception to find something to write with, staying on the line with Joe and Samaria who confess that they're okay without Dad in the room, because this isn't the first time he's left them on their own since they got there. I don't know whether to laugh or cry when I relay the tragicomical situation to Doug and Hils. In the end, we decide it would be better to laugh, as long as the children are okay.

Deli comes to stay with me during that weekend to celebrate her birthday and share her recent relationship woes over a few bottles of wine. I listen to her and ensure she's well fed, cooking her favourite noodle dish and encouraging her to be true to her heart. Advice that is easy to give but hard to follow when it comes to myself. Before she leaves for her next filming session as one of the actors in a long-running Welsh soap opera, she thanks me

for looking after her, not just over this weekend, but during the dark days following her dad's death in our second year at uni. I don't remember, but she recounts how I would get her out of bed every day to attend lectures, cook for her, make her laugh and hold her close when she needed it. With tears welling up in my eyes, I tell her that's what friends are for, to be the light that others need in their moments of darkness. Deli hugs me close and says in the gentlest voice,

"Simone, you are the quietest you've ever been in the eighteen years I've known you. You were always proud to be loud! I don't know what has happened to silence you; all I know is, you deserve to be happy. Find your voice again dearest, and choose to be with the people who will love you and listen when your heart speaks."

My tears fall freely after I close the front door, full of regret at the choices I've made, wishing fervently that I could choose all over again. Above all else, I know in my heart that the only things I wouldn't change are the choices I made to have my precious children.

Chapter 11
Should I Stay or Should I Go

The Straw that Broke the Camel's Back

SIX MONTHS LATER, Dave is happy now he has started building our house extension. I take the last two weeks in August off, going on holiday with the children to the Gower peninsula, so Dave can work full-time on the house. We have a wonderful time

away, walk for miles, and enjoy the picture-postcard, chalk-white sand beaches that remind me of being in the Caribbean, just a tad chillier.

After a long drive home on the Saturday just before the August bank holiday, we arrive home to get changed for a 30th birthday barbeque taking place in Eastham village where the children's best friends live. Dave demands sex when I'm taking a quick shower, but I say no because we are already late. This puts him in a foul mood, so he starts drinking as soon as we get there; I stay sober because I will be driving home later that evening.

The party goes on for a while on the village green until it's way past the little ones' bedtime. When it gets to 10pm, I look for Dave everywhere so we can go home. Joe and Samaria are already strapped into their car seats and nodding off. Eventually, I see him emerging from one of the houses just off the village green, followed shortly afterwards by a rather large lady who I vaguely recognise as one of the other school mums. Dave gets in the passenger seat looking guilty and defiant at the same time.

I ask him what he was doing in her house and he claims he went to look at something she was giving away because her son no longer needed it. I don't believe him but stifle my suspicions and questions because of the children. Once they're both tucked up in bed, I ask him to be honest but he goes on the offensive, grabs me by the throat, pins me up against the wall and tells me to shut up, reminding me of the time in Carterton after I found the girl's name and number in his jacket pocket. The time when I ended up concussed in A&E at the John Radcliffe Hospital after he used my head as a punch bag. I stop questioning him.

The following night, I trick Dave into admitting his infidelity by claiming that one of the other mums witnessed the dirty deed through her neighbouring window. Busted, he is completely unrepentant, instead blaming me for what he did, dismissing it as just getting rid of the dirty water because I refused to have sex with him before the party. He tells me that it's been a long time coming, that I'm not feminine enough, not slim enough (the irony considering she is at least four times my size), that I have bigger balls than him and he feels emasculated. Unable to process his betrayal and anxious to avoid a repeat of last night's violence, I drive to Robin's house, which is close to our Milton Keynes office. Robin says to stay as long as I need to as it's just him in his 4-bedroom house, but I know I will eventually go back to be with the children.

OVER THE NEXT week, I travel in between Hull and Milton Keynes for work, wearing a silk scarf to hide the bruises, confiding only in Doug, Hils and Robin the true extent of my relationship breakdown. Hils is super supportive, especially after she discovers that her husband has been having a sordid affair with a Russian gold-digger. We become firm friends, supporting each other through the disintegration of our respective relationships.

Dave and I have not slept in the same bed since Joe was born, because both children sleep better when I am sandwiched closely between them. Now, I can't even bring myself to have any physical contact with Dave, because I realise that I can no longer trust him. Mama and Mum would often tell me to be careful when carrying glasses of water because spilt water can't be gathered up: as the Chinese saying goes 覆水难收 (fù shuǐ nán shōu)[57]. Dave has well and truly shattered the illusion that he loves me and I can no longer gather up what remains of our broken marriage.

Before I leave for Singapore with the children in December to spend Christmas with my parents, leaving Dave in Tenbury Wells to finish off the extension, he tells me to get over myself and my huge ego, to accept that it was just a blow-job and meant nothing. He fully expects me to return in the new year ready to resume our relationship as his dutiful wife.

---

57. 覆水难收: spilt water can't be gathered up.

#

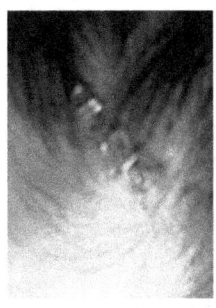

I KNOW NOW that I should have left him after he first hit me in London when Mary and I caught him with the girl he left Vicky for. I stayed to help him because I cared about him more than I cared about myself. I realise now what a poor choice it was, sitting in the consultation room of the top neurosurgeon in Singapore. He tells me that UK doctors are too laid back, that he recommends operating to remove the lump growing in towards my brain just above my right temple. He believes it is the cause of all the migraines I've suffered from, over the twelve years since 1995 when Dave punched me in the nose and head, creating ingrowing calcification as the skull fracture healed.

I spend Christmas Eve morning in surgery, reluctantly leaving Joe and Beanie in my parents' care. I return to convalesce at their home later that night, looking like Frankenstein's monster with blood trickling down my face from the stapled wound. The operation rounds up a dreadful few months, not helped by mediating to prevent World War III breaking out between Mum and Pa, staying strong for Joe and Beanie, who are understandably upset by the sight of my head wound, and Dave calling to say he misses us and finally being contrite, turning on the waterworks and begging me not to end our marriage.

The only saving grace is my almost daily MSN Messenger chats with Doug, who despite being 6,753 miles away from me, is the person I feel closest to and who I trust implicitly. Even though we're stupidly loyal to our partners and haven't physically engaged because of our staunch values and consciences, I know he is my soul mate — showing through his actions, concern for me, and careful listening what true love really is. I give him my heart for safekeeping, trusting him to be careful with it.

\#

WHEN THE CHILDREN and I return to the UK in early 2008, Dave is there to ferry us home. He looks at the scar on my head and says absolutely nothing to acknowledge the hurt he caused. I realise once again how little I actually mean to him, how I've wasted fourteen years of my life on someone who only wants me for what I can do for him, not for who I actually am. I carry on regardless at work, masking the worsening situation at home because 家丑不可外扬 (jiā chǒu bù kě wài yáng)[58]. Mum and Pa taught me through their example how family shames can't be taken outside, and I know better than to wash my dirty linen in public. At our annual office Christmas party in Hull (always held in mid-January to keep costs down), the smile on my face belies the turmoil I feel within. Only Doug and Hils know the true extent of the dilemma I struggle with, how Guilt keeps me firmly anchored in my unhappy marriage, while Self-Love pleads with me to flee for self-preservation.

Lesley calls regularly from New Zealand. Having escaped

---

58. 家丑不可外扬: Family shames can't be taken outside.

a physically violent, toxic relationship twenty years ago, she is worried sick and truly understands how difficult this decision is. I'm reminded of Mama urging me to always be kind because brave faces hide broken hearts. I am grateful for the kindness of my closest friends, once strangers who took the time to really listen when I replied to their customary conversation opener of "How are you?" I've learned never to ask anyone that question unless I am truly interested in listening to what they wish to share. I've learned over decades of working well with people the importance of listening to understand, not to reply.

BY MAY 2008, Dave has finished the extension. Because I'm rarely there to tether him to normality, he starts to unravel and has now fallen out with our closest neighbours. Val tells me that they've had to get a court injunction to keep him away due to his aggressive and threatening behaviour over a trivial hedge-trimming dispute. She also shares her worry that he's endangering the children's safety because she's seen him pulling them behind his car in an open-top trailer, without anything to prevent them from falling out, driving at breakneck speed up and down the rough gravel driveway. More often than not, the children wander up unaccompanied to their house; she's kind enough to feed them and escort them to the edge of our garden afterwards. She's seen them climb unsupervised to the top of the scaffolding left over from the newly finished extension and worries for their safety. I try to speak with Dave about the need to be the responsible adult, to hold things together for Joe and Beanie, but he brushes off my attempts and changes the subject to us.

After several months of zero physical contact, Dave tries to salvage our relationship with uncomfortably forced hugs and unwanted massages. He tells me we'll never be happy if we stay in the UK, and wants me to explore Canada or France as our next happy place. Looking back over the many moves we've made, I finally see the pattern of our lives, in the same way as batsmen would learn which bowlers they struggled against by studying the multi-coloured cricket score cards I used to create. I realise Dave will never be happy wherever we go, because he is unable to prevent the deep discontent within him from spilling out and spreading like uncontrolled cancer to tarnish the lives of the people around him. With help from Doug and Hils, I start to plan our escape, learning how to walk on the knife-edge, acutely aware of how unhinged Dave is and how he could snap if I move too quickly. Dave's desperation increases when he senses how close I am to leaving him. He calls incessantly when I'm away with work and even tries to write.

I leave my job and start a new one with Virgin Media working out of their Birmingham office to cut down on travel, so I can spend more time with the children. I agree to go for counselling at Relate, but after a preliminary one-to-one consultation, when I admit Dave's been sporadically violent in the past, they tell me they can continue to speak with me only, not Dave because they are not equipped to deal with domestic violence. They refer Dave to RESPECT but he refuses to go because he doesn't want to be labelled as a wife-beater.

After his letter, he forces himself on me just once, and only refrains from repeating the rape when I tell him that our GP has recorded the incident as non-consensual intercourse after prescribing the morning-after pill; how he has urged me to report the rape to the police. Since then, I know he's been on various dating websites and I suspect he's had sexual liaisons with other women, a relief for me, although I feel concern that these women may suffer the same fate.

Dear Simone,
I've just put the phone down from you and poured a whisky. I don't know what to say but will try. I phoned because I remember when we first met and the long phone conversations we had. I miss you now like I missed you in Singapore (you just phoned). I know how much I've hurt you and betrayed the friendship we've always had. You are and always will be my best friend. I've never told you how happy I was when you came back from Singapore and moved in with me. I suppose I was too engrossed in my own self pity, everything we have now is down to the kids & because of you. I don't care about the house, it's you & the kids that mean everything to me. I'm getting off track, fuck me herbs letter must have taken some writing. I don't know why I did what I did, didn't even fancy the fat bitch, and the stupid things I said after,

was just bollocks, I don't know if I was just trying to hurt you or it was the drink or or your on the defience go on the attack, I dont sensed that we had'nt been close for a while and I really miss that. Like you said the knife incident in NZ didn't help, you have to understand that until you told me about it I had forgotten about it (Joe's coughing) (beer 5th). ...
I'll do anything to keep our marriage alive. Counselling, therapy lobotomy, castration, did I really change well Sam was born, She means the world to me, I suppose I wanted a older boy at first but that didn't last long, I know I've never been much of a kisser, I don't think we got too many when I was younger, but I'd like to learn

were both under pressure & the kids are suffering as a result we never meant it to be like this or I don't think we'd'v have moved back we don't seem to do things as a family which is what we both want they grow so fast we have to make the most of them, I haven't eaten and the whisky is kicking in but I love you Simone I know I don't show it to well, it's my self loathing uptraying can you give me another chance to show I can be a proper person

P.S. I never meant what I said about it's made round to go round I'm insanely jealous really

Think of the Children

A YEAR AFTER that fateful barbecue, I receive a call from Joe and Samaria while I'm at work, both crying hysterically and asking me to come home quickly. It turns out that Joe had inadvertently closed the lounge door on Beanie's finger, unaware that she was walking behind him. I calm them both down and ascertain that Beanie is okay if still a little sore. They sound terrified though. Upon probing, I find out that Dave lost his temper, effing and blinding at Joe, slapped him, then dragged him up the stairs, kicking and screaming, by his right arm. Samaria chose to stay with her brother to comfort him. They tell me Dad has locked them in my office and they saw him drive off somewhere.

I'm relieved that they're physically okay, and proud that they remembered how to use the speed dial buttons like I taught them for emergency situations like this. I'm deeply concerned that Dave's violence is now being directed at our kids. I don't care what happens to me, but I have to protect my children and bring them up in a psychologically safe environment. This incident reminds me of my childhood with Mum and Pa smashing our bedroom mirrors. I tell myself that my choices have to be better from now on, to protect my children so they can thrive.

#

IT'S SEPTEMBER 2008, a month after Dave's violence towards Joe, when I finally tell Dave that it's over. We're in the garden of The Fountain pub overlooking the rolling rural landscape while Joe and Beanie play on the children's climbing frame. We've driven there in separate cars because he has a job to look at afterwards. Overcome with sadness and regret, I cry as I confirm what we both already know.

"I'm sorry Dave. I just can't do this anymore. We need to go our separate ways because we're both deeply unhappy and it's beginning to affect the kids. We'll sell the house, work out the finances amicably and of course, the children will live with me. You can still see them though. We'll work out a plan to ensure you have them for at least fifty percent of the time, alternate weekends maybe. Whatever works for you." I look at him fearfully, wondering which Dave will respond, Mr Sad, Mr Angry or Mr Someone Else, unsurprised when he doesn't turn on the waterworks.

He spits out his reply with cold bitterness, "So after you've leached everything out of me, you're just going to leave me a husk and deprive the children of their father. I suppose you think I'm going to be a chump and babysit your brats while you find a new boyfriend. Well, you can fuck off if you think I'm that stupid!"

I'm suddenly thankful that we're in a public place, because I can see his fists clenching tightly and beginning to twitch towards me, his eyes now glacial-blue with icy rage. I see him clocking that there are other people in the garden. He checks himself before he wheels around and storms off to his car, setting off with such speed that the screeching tyres kick up a dust cloud from the deep grooves he's left in the gravel and my heart. Filled with a sense of foreboding, I call Joe and Samaria over before heading home.

THAT NIGHT, WITH several more in the following months, heralds the start of unprecedented and escalating violence from Dave. Having lost hope of rekindling our relationship, he loses it big time and the children increasingly wake up to find police officers in the house on the occasions when he's so drunk, I'm afraid he'll do more than choke me. With help from Hils and Doug, I consult with estate agents to put the house on the market and with a solicitor about divorce proceedings. Fate thwarts a quick exit, the global credit crunch sending the UK into its worst recession for nearly eighty years. We struggle to find a buyer for the house and can't afford to live apart because childcare is so expensive. I keep going till October 2009, somehow managing to pay for everything and surviving life with an unpredictable sociopath. During these turbulent thirteen months, Autopilot Me is mainly in charge because it's the only way I can cope with Dave's extreme and erratic behaviour.

Dave goes from tearful tantrums, when he pleads with me not to break up our family and deprive the children of their father, to angry outbursts where he holds me captive in a neck hold, controlling the strength of his squeeze so as not to leave any tell-tale marks that would incriminate him. I hear from one of our local police constables, Nick, a gentle giant with a big heart, that Dave is now known in our community as Mr Angry. This is after a visit to caution him for reckless driving where he nearly ran over a young girl riding her pony along the country lanes. They also warn him to wind his neck in after handling multiple complaints from dissatisfied customers he's threatened with physical violence, when they've demanded refunds for shoddy building work. Unhinged, Dave becomes verbally abusive to the children's teachers and football coach, earning himself bans from entering the school and football club.

Our divorce is finalised in May 2009 after a long and protracted negotiation where Dave threatens to sue for custody of Joe and Samaria if I don't give him fifty percent of the house equity. I finally agree to a 53:47 split despite my solicitor advising against it, because I'm more concerned about my children than money. Dave starts being openly rude to my parents, Hils and Lesley when he answers the telephone before I can get to it. The situation is becoming untenable — there are incidents where he tries to control my every move by confiscating my house and car keys. Dave says he can't wait to sell the house so "I can get as far away as possible from you! You lazy, useless bitch!" Yet he turns down the only offer we get from a prospective buyer for the house in May, claiming it won't give him enough money to move on. We avoid each other where possible; he leaves as soon as I get home from work and sleeps in the old part of the house, while the children and I sleep in the new extension. At weekends, he disappears and sometimes doesn't return till the early hours on Monday morning. I don't ask questions, relieved at not having to walk on eggshells all the time.

Now he's gone more often, I can see how damaged both Joe and Beanie are. Samaria refuses to speak to strangers without using Joe or myself as her spokesperson. When she does speak, she whispers in a heartbreakingly hushed voice. Her close friend Catherine stopped coming around because, apparently, her mum does not approve of Dave. She's also been waking up with nightmares where she sees Dad feeding pieces of my body to Great White sharks. They stick Finding Nemo stickers on my filing cabinet to "save Mummy from the scary sharks", and tape a note to my office door that says 'NO FIGHTING' to warn Dad off. I'm told by one of the school mums that Joe tried to throttle his best friend Ella after she said something he didn't like when they were trampolining; I know he's witnessed Dave choking me. Sometimes, when I refuse to let him have more sweets,

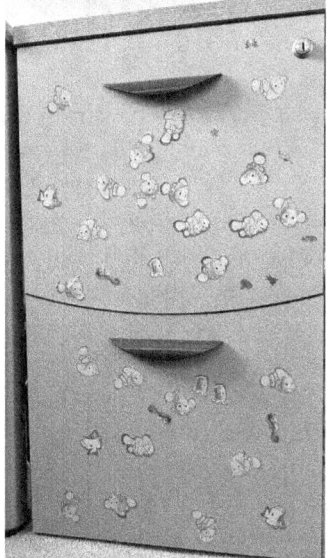

he becomes angry and shouts out that I'm lazy and useless. I am heartbroken at their loss of innocence, feeling guilty once again.

Dave reneges on our agreement to rent out the property indefinitely if we can't find a buyer. He can see I am desperate to get the children away from him and begins to rant at me when he comes home drunk from the pub, instead of going to his bedroom. During these alcohol-fuelled rages, he accuses me of poisoning the children against him, tells me I am always too critical of him, that I act all superior to him, and I'm such a stuck-up snobbish bitch. He threatens to keep going the next time he chokes me. He claims he is happy to go to prison because he's already lost everything.

I reach out to my solicitor for help, so she steps in to remind Dave that the financial consent order, agreed during divorce proceedings, mandates that 'the wife shall have conduct of the sale'. She warns him against further threatening behaviour towards me and the estate agents, who fear him. The letter is sent via his solicitors in early October. I've already made arrangements to rent out our house. With Doug's help, I am choosing a new school for the children and which property to rent in Cambridgeshire. I've also organised my transfer to Virgin Media's Hertfordshire branch.

Five days after the letter is sent, I come home to find that Dave has already gone without waiting for me to return, leaving Joe and Samaria alone in the dark lounge. I notice the solicitor's letter ripped into pieces, the shreds strewn across the hallway. I can feel his residual rage lingering ominously around us, but turn on all the lights to cheer everyone up, make the children's tea, get them ready and settled for bed, before retiring to my office to send emails to the letting agents.

Just before midnight, I hear loud crashes downstairs in the hallway. I check that the office door is locked. I hold my breath when I hear his heavy footsteps thumping up the stairs. The floorboards outside my office creak when the footsteps pause. Then I hear them move away towards the back bedroom and exhale in relief. Too soon though, because now they're thundering back towards my office. Dave kicks the door down, bursting in with his bloodshot, glacial-blue eyes, all glazed over with the red mist of rage, smelling like a brewery, smelling of Pa just before he whacked Mum. I turn to retreat into the bedroom and manage to lock the door before he gets to me.

Enraged by my temporary escape, I hear him lift the heavy wooden desk and tip it over on its side, before he breaks through the bedroom door roaring like an enraged animal. "You can't get away that easily you bitch! I'm going to show you who's boss! And you're going to get what's coming to you, YOU FUCKING CUNT!" He drags me back into the office by my hair, throws me against the uprooted desk, slamming my shoulder into the corner between the desk and cabinet, wedging me into the small gap so I can't move, my cheek pressed up against multiple colourful Nemos. His hands wring my neck, choking the life out of me till I feel like I'm going to pass out. As he bites down on my lips and bruises them with a cruel controlling kiss, I can feel his raging hard-on. I hear myself think I'll be lucky if all he does is rape me. I struggle for breath, painfully aware of Joe and Beanie's loud, wailing voices coming from the bedroom. Suddenly full of supernatural strength, I bring my knee up into his groin, somehow managing to push him off. While he's bent over in pain, I grab the cordless telephone, run back into the bedroom, dragging the office chair with me, so I can wedge the door shut. I dial 999 and collapse onto the carpet, cuddling my babies close, holding onto them tightly until we all stop sobbing.

THE NEXT NINETEEN days fly past in a flurry of fear and furious activity. After scouring the nearby countryside, Dave is found hiding in the bushes and arrested for assault. I call in sick because everyone at work is still unaware of my domestic situation. I go to court to seek protection for the children and myself. Within a day, a Non-Molestation Order is in place alongside a Court Injunction that forbids Dave from being within 100 metres of me.

I pay for all the locks to be changed to prevent Dave from re-entering the house. A wise choice because on the day he is released on bail, I find the conservatory doors jemmied open and signs of attempted forced entry from the conservatory via the hallway door. I spend every single one of those nineteen nights lying awake in fear that he will come back to finish what he started. With help from some of the school mums, my neighbours and friends, I manage to get the children to school, go to work, pack for our move across the UK, move Dave's belongings into the outdoor garage for him to collect once we are gone, and clean the property so it is ready for the new tenants.

On 24 October 2009, feeling almost entirely exhausted but still a tiny bit hopeful, I bundle up my babies, along with dreams of a more peaceful life, into my car and drive across the country to try again.

Interlude 6

As you join me on my journey, please take a musical break and listen to the song that captures the mood of that particular moment in time. Or read on.

The choice is yours.

'Human', *song from the album 'Head or Heart'*
by Christina Perri, released November 2013

Chapter 12
Prince Charming

I ALWAYS THOUGHT that True Love would announce herself triumphantly with great fanfare, once she had vanquished the selfish desires driving the men in my life to bend me to their will for their own benefit. Call it naivety, gullibility, or just wanting to believe there's good in everyone, but I find it hard to comprehend how anyone can knowingly manipulate other people with empty rhetoric, only to sacrifice them like unsuspecting pawns to win the endgame of self-gratification. Doug and I spend many an evening after work listening to each other's experiences of love, learning that the secret to happy relationships is finding the balance between Yin and Yang, between selfless giving and self-centred taking.

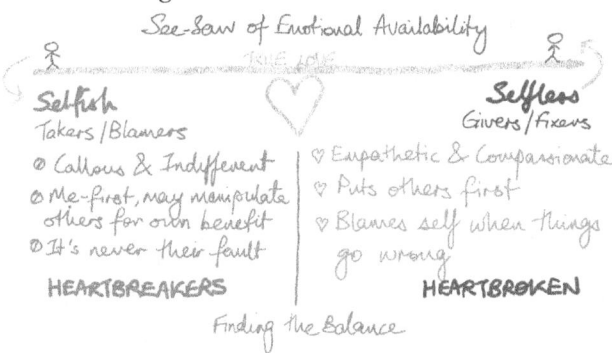

See-Saw of Emotional Availability

Selfish — Takers/Blamers
- Callous & Indifferent
- Me-first, may manipulate others for own benefit
- It's never their fault

HEARTBREAKERS

Selfless — Givers/Fixers
- Empathetic & Compassionate
- Puts others first
- Blames self when things go wrong

HEARTBROKEN

Finding the Balance

Doug is fortunate to have been born to Glaswegian parents in straight-talking Newcastle. Unlike my disruptive parents, Jean and Eric Warren epitomise a harmonious union of hearts and minds, bringing up a son who knows how to love himself and others in equal balance. After our fateful first meeting, we discover how East and West aren't that much different, and are delighted to share the same values and beliefs despite having lived vastly varied lives. Whether we're working on the business improvement think-tank or talking about music, that feeling of fatedness finds us confiding in each other in equal measure. Doug shares his disappointment at choosing to walk away from twenty-six years of living with a narcissist when he realised that she didn't care about his needs and wants, or love him for who he was. She had selected him for what he could do for her and how he made her feel. Not long after they were married twenty-three years ago, he overheard her telling her mum when asked if she'd done the right thing marrying him, 'He's not the best, but he'll do'.

During the messy divorce proceedings in the spring of 2008, I escape with the children for a weekend at Hardwick Hall and Bolsover Castle, because I want them to grow up believing in the existence of true love, chivalry and noble hearts. I am anxious for both Joe and Samaria to experience what a normal loving relationship looks like, so I invite Doug to join us on Saturday. My heart fills with happiness when, after lunch at the Hardwick Inn, the three of them giggle unaffectedly while playing tag, running from stone to stone as if they've known each other forever, instead of having met an hour ago. My beautiful Beanie, aged four, precocious and petite, doesn't complain once and gamely walks for miles, climbing to the top of one of the turreted towers at Bolsover where she declares she will stay until Prince Charming comes to rescue her. The romantic in me tears up, wanting to perpetuate the illusion, hoping against hope that life will be kinder to her than it has been to me; while the experienced cynic mutters inaudibly, *Don't hold your breath Beanie, because you'll just turn blue.* Optimistic me puts the cynic in her place: *It's taken me thirty-six years to find him, but I know deep in my heart that Doug Warren is my Prince Charming. So, you need to hush.*

I watch him while he teaches Joe to sword-fight, his Royal Marine training coming in handy, and when he gives the now-tired Samaria a piggy-back to the car. Both children plead with 'Duckie' (so named because Samaria can't pronounce the G) to stay with us overnight but we know that would be inappropriate, so he just stays for dinner instead.

That night while the children are asleep, I think back to Halloween when Doug first told me about his failed marriage to give me hope that I could survive mine, encouraging me to keep the faith. Feeling his pain mirrored in my heart, I place my hand on top of his to comfort him. I'm surprised to feel like a thirteen-year-old all over again, excitement coursing through my veins, the searing heat of desire spreading from our entwined hands straight through to my heart and deep down inside. We're so lost in each other's eyes, gazing soul-to-soul, I know he feels our interconnection too. At twilight in the pub car park, when we go to hug and kiss each other goodbye on the cheek, our lips meet instead. I feel his love as he lingers for the longest time, before we both throw caution to the wind, immersed in the intensity of raw emotion as tears of suppressed longing flow freely. It's as if I've never been kissed before, like I'm finally meeting the nameless stranger of my teenage dreams. Everything fades into non-existence; I've been transported to an other-worldly haven, a paradise lost so many years ago but found again, here and now. I feel his hot hands on my skin, reaching under and up towards my heart, pulling me so close you wouldn't be able to tell where I stop and he begins; I'm touching him too, responding with equal passion, yearning for him to throw me onto the car bonnet with wild abandon, so we can both feel alive again. Doug's kiss speaks volumes without words. For the first time in my life, I feel like I'm enough, just as I am.

"Oh, I say!" We surface to hear that shocked exclamation from a group of OAPs[59] standing next to us. We've been lost in each other for so long that the dark night shadows have banished the surreal silhouettes of twilight. Smiling shyly like a sentimental schoolgirl, I've never felt so enlightened in my life. We've found each other at last and I feel sure that Doug's unconditional love will light my way home to happiness. I realise that True Love doesn't always trumpet her arrival with fireworks and fanfare. Sometimes she slips in surreptitiously when least expected, long after I stopped looking for her and just when I needed her most.

I WOULD LOVE to say that everything went smoothly after the children and I arrived in St Neots eight days before my fortieth birthday. I would love to lie, but we all know that life has a way of throwing curve-balls until you become an expert at bending your mind to learn the lessons, re-think your approach and make better choices.

We stay at Doug's flat the first night, having run out of time to unpack at our nearby rental property. We're in a celebratory mood and share a Thai takeaway, both children relaxed and comfortable in his company. But that night, Joe continues his pattern of being sick and bed-wetting, and Samaria stays silent or whispers. I wonder despairingly if they will ever recover from those years of seeing too much too soon. Eventually, with support from teaching and counselling staff at Great Paxton CE Primary School, Joe and Beanie settle into their new school and make new friends. I, however, struggle to pay for childcare, the mortgage on our Tenbury Wells property, and the house rental in St Neots, trying my best to juggle the demands of being a working mum and single parent, with Dave disregarding the court order by not paying any child support. Doug supports us through his actions — teaching both children how to ride their bikes without stabilisers, helping to fix things when they break, and just being

---

59. OAPs: British abbreviation for Old Age Pensioners.

there whenever we need anything. Six months later, it's a relief when he agrees to move in with us after the children beg him to, because he has become the rock around which our lives are anchored. I'm reminded of my Uncle Donald, a man of few words, who always showed his love rather than speaking of it.

Dave is noticeably absent from the children's lives, seeing them for a measly total of thirteen days out over the next twelve months, despite me trying my best to encourage contact. Joe, though much calmer than when he first arrived, still worries us by being very physical during playground disputes, but I work closely with the school to agree a restorative approach which focuses on fixing the behaviour rather than punishing the child.

One weekend, Joe, now eight, pulls me aside, asking me in a low voice how he can stop the bad half of him ('that comes from Dad') from hurting other people when he feels angry. He thinks that the part of him which comes from me is the good half, but isn't always strong enough to overcome the bad half from Dad. Knowing how intrigued he is by science, I explain that parents provide DNA which determines characteristics like his eye and hair colour, but those twenty-three pairs of chromosomes do not think things through or make decisions for him. I share with him the Cherokee legend of the two wolves. Happy again, Joe's eyes widen with the realisation that he can choose how he wants to behave, he can choose which wolf to feed. Samaria, silent for so long, is still shy when she meets people for the first time, but is growing in confidence, and shares the same love of Galaxy chocolate and chips as her Duckie. I honestly do not know what we would do without him. Having had no one to depend on for

There is a battle of two wolves inside us all.

One is evil: it is anger, jealousy, greed, resentment, lies, inferiority and ego.

The other is good: it is joy, peace, love, hope, humility, kindness, empathy and truth.

The wolf that wins? The one you feed.

so long, Doug is such a pleasant shock to the system, although a small part of me still wonders what he will do when he sees through my facade.

#

IN JULY 2010, Dave uses legal aid to fund an application for court-ordered contact with the children when they refuse to go with him on a two-week holiday abroad. I am astounded by his decision because over the nine months since our move, he's chosen not to have contact despite me encouraging him to, and when he does, he spends all his time interrogating the children about me and asking, 'Does Mummy have a new boyfriend?' Over the next nineteen months, he drags us through the Family Court, culminating in court-ordered psychological assessments, portraying himself as the victim of a vendetta by me to poison the children against him. He refuses to speak with me or attend family mediation. During court proceedings (where he is supported by his legal team, while I represent myself as I can't afford legal representation, but earn too much for legal aid), he always tries to speak over me when it is my turn to answer questions. So much so that the Family Court judge tells him to let me speak, and despite the stressful situation, I choke back a giggle when she commands him to do 'less transmit, more receive'.

The psychological assessment highlights that Dave exhibits signs of antisocial personality disorder (associated with sociopaths), while I have a compulsion to portray myself in the best possible light, and 'this may have been influenced by cultural factors that promote extreme conscientiousness'. It's clear that Western psychologists have little to no understanding of the Eastern societal view that family secrets must be kept private to avoid shame, and one should always suffer in silence. This whole soul-destroying process ends on Joe's tenth birthday when Dave returns them late which means Joe misses his own birthday party. The court washes its hands of the whole sorry matter after Dave divulges the contents of the psychological assessment, using it to disparage me by telling the children about my teenage pregnancy and what happened to my first baby, saying "Mum doesn't want you and she'll get rid of you too. She only cares about herself and her career". Doug holds us together through all of this, his love and strength shielding us from more harm — he is our safe haven and shelter in the storm.

NOT LONG AFTER, we visit my parents in Singapore and they come with us on a family holiday to Penang. I have already warned Doug about my dysfunctional family, but he needs to see it for himself to believe it. Samaria unwittingly becomes the catalyst for another family catastrophe when we're squeezed together in a lift with a bickering couple. After they exit on their floor, Grandpa, who's clearly irritated by their squabbling, grumbles loudly, "Some people never learn. He shouldn't speak to his wife like that in front of other people. We don't need to listen to that!"

Our usually quiet but always observant Beanie, wise beyond her years, lights the blue touch paper when she pipes up innocently, "But Grandpa, you can't say that because you always speak to Mama like that." Doug and I exchange a glance, both trying to suppress a smile at the insightful observations of our precocious eight-year-old who's going on eighty. Grandpa erupts. Mama defends her granddaughter. We spend the rest of the evening apologising for Samaria's apparent disrespect for her elders and mediating between my parents, who are once again contemplating divorce. We explain to Samaria that although she is spot on, it probably wasn't a good idea to speak the truth, out of respect for her grandparents. Doug does his best to play his part as UN peacekeeping ambassador, but I know my parents are polar opposites compared to his own, and that this will end as it always does. Mum and Pa will resign themselves to sticking with each other like a pair of rusty rivets.

To celebrate our first kiss-versary on Halloween and my birthday in November, Doug whisks me away to Venice for a child-free weekend. Ever the romantic, he takes me to the Bistrot de Venise for a special birthday meal where he presents me with my favourite yellow roses, a heart-shaped cake following a delightful meal from their Romantic menu and a diamond eternity ring. "Please will you marry me?" he asks hopefully, holding my hand with the ring poised over my finger. His thoughtful planning and unconditional love for me render me speechless. I can't believe he wants to marry me knowing what a complicated life I've lived. I wonder if I'm good enough to deserve such happiness and the love of a genuinely good man. I am deep in thought and keep him waiting for so long that he finally prompts, eyes twinkling mischievously, "Well, is it a yes or is it a no?"

"Yes. Of course I will." With happy tears falling as we kiss, my hand over his as we slide the eternity ring onto my ring finger, I feel his love permeate through my vein, the one which runs directly into my heart from my ring finger. I am reminded of what Rochester says to Jane, the most romantic line I've ever read: 'I have a strange feeling with regard to you: as if I had a string somewhere under my left ribs, tightly knotted to a similar string in you. And if you were to leave I'm afraid that cord of communion would snap. And then I've a notion that I'd take to bleeding inwardly'.

"Yes. A thousand times yes" I affirm, fervently

grateful. The little girl in me whispers, *But I'm afraid that you'll leave when you see how flawed I am. Please, please don't ever leave me because I don't think I could bear any more heartbreak.*

I FIND OUT that Doug has been planning this proposal since our Easter holiday to Singapore and Malaysia. He actually asked Pa formally for my hand in marriage after the Penang eruption, and also sought approval from Joe and Beanie. The little tinkers were in on the secret and I'm impressed that they managed to keep it quiet for over seven months.

On 7 July 2013, three days after Doug's birthday, we marry at Lumley Castle in the company of Doug's family and our closest friends. Joe is Doug's Best Man; Samaria and Hils' daughters (Karis and Gemma) my beautiful bridesmaids. Hils and Lesley read perfectly poignant prose during the ceremony. Our guests remark how everything about the day is unusual: our red, purple and black gothic attire, the 25 degree heat in North East England, Andy Murray winning his first ever Wimbledon Mens Singles trophy, the usual wedding hymns replaced by rock and gothic music

(Muse, The Cure, Evanescence, The Mission), Bilbo the barn owl flying down the aisle to deliver our wedding rings to Joe, the flamboyant master of ceremonies, Lord James, the harpist serenading us during the wedding breakfast, the magician who entertains our guests while they explore the castle grounds, Aerosmith's 'I Don't Want to Miss a Thing' as our first dance song, the disco with the eclectic music we love, Deli singing a Brazilian love song 'Sobre Todas as Coisas', while holding my hand on the steps of the Baron's Hall, and the musical fireworks display while the twilight stars shine over the happiest day of my life.

The ultimate highlight of the day is Doug's speech, which he delivers completely from memory, having spent months practising in front of our bedroom mirror and in conference rooms at work. His speech is another well-kept secret, surprising everyone, including me, with its wit and funny anecdotes, full of unabashedly sentimental emotion. It reduces everyone to tears, including our male guests who complain about the high pollen count making their eyes water so effusively. He allays all my fears with his heartfelt words,

"I would personally like to thank Stephen and Theresa for bringing up a daughter who is loving, thoughtful, kind, generous, always places everyone else's interests before her own, always goes the extra mile, and never utters one word of complaint. Simone, I would like to say in front of our distinguished guests that … you are the only person, who can ignite my imagination, keep pace with my passion, understand and embrace my emotions. You are the only one I want and need, and so, I choose to look no further, for I knew you were the one all those years ago, to whom I will stay forever loyal, steadfast and true. You don't have to jump through hoops of fire, perform death defying acts or

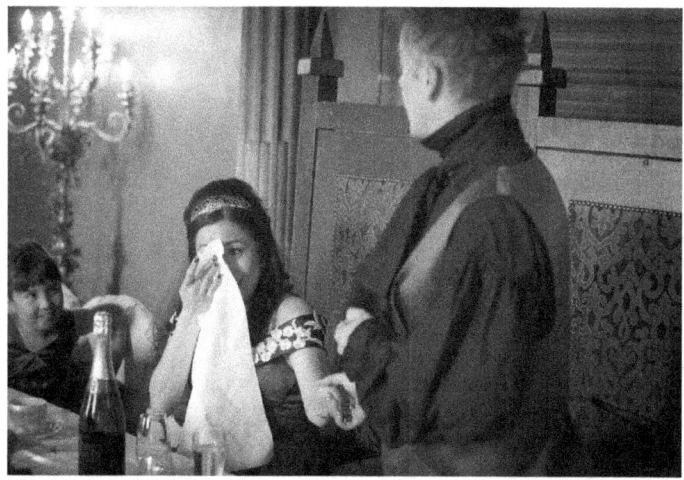

walk on water in order to impress ... for I love you just the way you are ...

With that in mind, I'd like to make three wishes, and have them all come true:

The first is a heartfelt wish of eternal happiness to you from this day forth. The second is a loving wish that life will always be as wonderful and good to you, as you have been to me. The third is a special wish that we will never be apart, and that you'll always share with me the love that's in your heart.

Finally, I'd like to say a thank you for giving that 'little boy behind the tree' his dreams back, but more importantly, helping him live those dreams. My Lords, Ladies and Gentlemen, please be upstanding, for the most important toast of all — to the Bride, to Simone."

There isn't a dry eye in the house. Overcome with emotion, I look back at the frogs I've kissed on my quest to find my Prince Charming and I know that for the first time, I've finally made the right choice.

#

THE NEXT NINE years bring more ups than downs for us all, or perhaps I'm just more able to cope now that I'm living with a fellow giver. We've both learnt not to fix anything we didn't break, just to listen and help when asked. Dave tries to make my life difficult during 'handovers' when he has contact with the children, but Doug is always there protecting us. As the children grow up, they decide, of their own accord, that they no longer wish to see their dad; Joe at fourteen and Samaria at fifteen. We live in a delightful townhouse one hundred and fifty metres from the river. Joe and Samaria are progressing well academically and emotionally, both daring to dream and working hard to achieve their ambitions. Doug travels with us to many far-flung locations, having taken more holidays abroad in the sixteen years since we first met, than he did during the twenty-six years with his ex-wife. But we also find pleasure and romance in the mundane ordinariness of everyday life. I enjoy volunteering and giving back to our local community, taking on responsibilities as parent governor, chair of the PTA at school and being on the management committee at our local football club, as well as managing Joe's grassroots football team for two years.

My career has gone from strength to strength, although I still prioritise my family over anything else — choosing a UK-based role with Microsoft, rather than travelling the world, while based out of China, with Jack Ma's Alibaba. Despite being offered a glamorous Global Partner Director role managing our relationships with global systems integrators and the 'Big 5' consulting firms, I didn't fancy being away from my family for eleven months out of twelve. So I end up managing a multi-million-pound business for Microsoft UK instead.

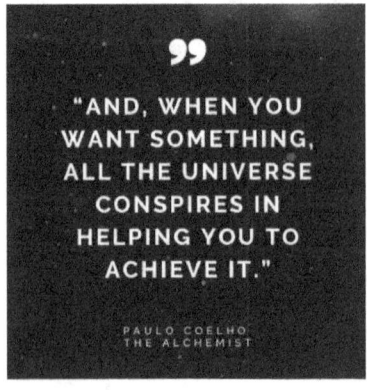

"AND, WHEN YOU WANT SOMETHING, ALL THE UNIVERSE CONSPIRES IN HELPING YOU TO ACHIEVE IT."

PAULO COELHO
THE ALCHEMIST

Yet, all is not right in my world. All those years of depression and stress-induced addiction have worn away my heart as constantly dripping water wears away stone (滴水穿石 dī shuǐ chuān shí)[60]. I feel fatigued, like a war-weary veteran who has survived numerous battles only to stumble and fall at the final hurdle. I start to experience chest pains but I ignore them, pushing through the pain and continuing to work long days, and sometimes, nights. My Apple watch ECGs[61] are normal so there's nothing to worry about, I tell myself. *Your heart is strong,* Courage reassures. But Sadness quips quietly, *Broken hearts need healing, Simone. You can't ignore me any longer. You need to heal.*

I don't listen to her because I am too busy to pause, because I don't deserve or want a pity party, and I know there are many poor souls out there who have suffered more than I have. I have so many blessings to count in my life, so I content myself with carrying on, grateful that life is finally being kind to me.

---

60. 滴水穿石: Dripping water wears away rock.

61. ECGs: Electrocardiograms (a simple test to check the heart's rhythm and electric activity).

Interlude 7

As you join me on my journey, please take a musical break and listen to the song that captures the mood of that particular moment in time. Or read on.

The choice is yours.

'Tower of Strength', *song from the album 'Children'*
by The Mission, released February 1988

Part Five
You & Me, Singapore & UK
(1987, 2022)

"(Love is) trust, responsibility, taking the weight for your choices and feelings, and spending the rest of your life living up to them. And above all, not hurting the object of your love."

William Parrish, 'Meet Joe Black' movie 1998,
based on the play La Morte in Vacanza by Alberto Casella

"Love is putting someone else's needs before yours."

Olaf the Snowman, 'Frozen' movie 2013
Inspired by 'The Snow Queen' by Hans Christian Andersen

Choices

In the early hours of 26 November 2022 after decades of carrying on regardless, I wake up with chest pains, a dead left arm and a racing heart. Doug drives me to A&E where they tell me my blood pressure is alarmingly high at a hypertensive crisis level of 206/170. Normal blood pressure is around 120/80. Faced with potential heart failure, after seventeen years of never taking a sick day, I decide it's time to listen to my body and book my sick leave straightaway. I also make appointments with a stress counsellor and one of the top cardiologists in the UK. My body is telling me she needs some long overdue TLC[62]. It's

BLOOD PRESSURE CATEGORY	SYSTOLIC mm Hg (upper number)		DIASTOLIC mm Hg (lower number)
NORMAL	LESS THAN 120	and	LESS THAN 80
ELEVATED	120 – 129	and	LESS THAN 80
HIGH BLOOD PRESSURE (HYPERTENSION) STAGE 1	130 – 139	or	80 – 89
HIGH BLOOD PRESSURE (HYPERTENSION) STAGE 2	140 OR HIGHER	or	90 OR HIGHER
HYPERTENSIVE CRISIS (consult your doctor immediately)	HIGHER THAN 180	and/or	HIGHER THAN 120

---

62. TLC: abbreviation for tender loving care.

time I listened.

We all make countless choices every day but so far, I can count on one hand the defining decisions that created a chain reaction of consequences so far-reaching as to span three and a half decades. So let's rewind to 1987, when I was seventeen, staring blankly out of the window, as Conscience and Common Sense joined my internal debate team to decide the future of my unborn child. In the end, neither one prevails; after several arduously indecisive hours, I instinctively open the Bible and the first words I read are from Psalm 127:3 —

> Children are a gift from the Lord; they are a real blessing.

I feel the lightbulb go off in my head; both Conscience and Common Sense are appeased and silent, now we've all managed to reach a compromise. In that moment, I fall to my knees and pray for the strength and courage to take my first step on the path less travelled. The first furrows of fear force their way up from deep down in my gut right up to behind my eyes. I'm afraid of angering and disappointing my parents, especially my mum, who has always warned me not to let men get me into trouble. *All men want is sex. Once they've had it, they'll treat you like dirt. So either you study hard and depend on yourself or you marry a rich man! Whatever you do, don't end up with a pauper who can't look after you! Love doesn't put food on the table or clothes on your back!* I can hear her voice echoing loudly inside me, my anxiety and dread building to fever pitch. *She's going to kill me*, I think, as panic takes over! *Maybe it's for the best*, chirps another voice flippantly, *at least then you won't live to suffer the consequences.*

On the night I tell them, I feel like a character in a tragicomedy. Pa has just returned from one of his business trips in India or Sri Lanka and Mum has just changed into her pyjamas after wolfing down her dabao[63] dinner. I feel bad because they both looked so tired and preoccupied. After several false starts, the words rush out of me in a sort of strangled scream, "I'm sorry, but I'm pregnant!". I look down at the cold, cream-coloured marble floor, wishing it would open up and swallow me whole.

"Whaaaattt did you say?" asks my dad incredulously, his body as frozen as mine, as if we are all playing some cruel game of musical chairs where I'm the class clown left standing in the spotlight. I repeat those five fateful words. I can't look at them but become aware of the now deafening silence. Mum has switched off her favourite Chinese drama where the female protagonist is threatening suicide after being jilted by her lover. My inner flippant fiend quips, *Maybe you should do the same!* It feels eerily calm, like the lull before the almighty storm.

Eventually Mum erupts. Pa tries to interject with how, what and why questions but it's impossible for either of us to interrupt her in full flow. I can't remember the exact words she spits out in her torrential tirade of rage and disbelief, but it's something along the lines of how stupid I am to get myself into this predicament, how could I, how dare I allow a disgusting man to take advantage of me, how could I, how much shame I'm bringing on our family, how could I, how we will be the laughing stock of Singapore, how could I, how my future will be ruined if we don't act quickly enough, how could I ... you get the gist. She frantically rifles through the Yellow Pages as she rants on and on.

"What are you doing?" Pa shouts angrily.

"I'm trying to find a private guy-nee[64] so we can get rid of it!" she fires back.

"STOP IT! Please just stop and listen to me. I'm not having an abortion. I'm keeping my baby." You can hear a pin drop in the stunned silence that follows.

---

63. Dabao: Literally translated as 'dry packet' - Hokkien word for takeaway food (noun) or buying takeaway food (verb).

64. Guy-nee: Singlish for Gynaecologist.

#

I WAIT IMPATIENTLY in front of KFC at Far East Plaza Shopping Centre. Adam is coming home from camp for the weekend and we need to talk before showdown time with my parents. When I first told him I was pregnant, he went from shocked disbelief to questioning if the baby was his (he's still suspicious about Sam), then finally to acceptance. He is very hesitant to tell his mum because he's just as afraid as I am of her reaction, especially as she thinks my mum is a snob and we come from incompatible backgrounds. He says that as a last resort, we can tell his Mum and move into his family home temporarily, but I know that five grown-ups and a new-born baby living in a cramped two-bedroom HDB[65] flat is a recipe for disaster. We've been having short, whispered telephone conversations late at night after my parents have gone to bed, but not enough to talk things through properly because there just aren't enough coins to feed the public telephone at camp. I am so deep in thought that I feel his strong arms wrap around me, enveloping me in his familiar scent of Drakkar Noir, before I see him. Sobs threaten to break free so I bury my face deep into his chest to keep them at bay. Public displays of affection are still frowned upon so we try hard not to draw unwanted scrutiny. We hurry into the familiar haunt of the stairwell, fairly private only because most Singaporeans prefer using lifts or escalators.

"What's happened?" Adam's concern only sets me off again, so he just holds me until I am all cried out. I regain enough composure to tell him what has happened over the fifteen hours since I dropped the bombshell. My mum has vacillated between concern, pragmatism and anger; neither of us got much sleep, so I'm not surprised at how events escalated as soon as I told her I was meeting Adam. She tried to stop me leaving the apartment, but was unable to physically restrain me, so she shoved me as I

---

65. HDB: Abbreviation for Housing Development Board (government-subsidised, usually high-rise, buildings).

turned to walk down the stairs. I tumbled halfway down before I was able to grab hold of the railings. The last words Mum said as I ran off crying were, "I hope you suffer a miscarriage, you stubborn, stubborn child!"

All I can think about is whether the baby was hurt, but Adam is incandescent with rage. I immediately regret telling him because we've agreed to go back to the apartment to meet with my parents this afternoon. I am in no fit state to play the part of UN peacekeeping ambassador and I can see how, with everyone's emotions running high, it will just end up being like Armageddon. Sadly, I'm right.

I FAIL MISERABLY at trying to keep the peace between my parents and Adam. My mum spends most of the time trying to hit him, enraged by how he has 'taken advantage' of her daughter, shouting and screaming at him like a banshee. My dad seethes silently. Adam tries valiantly to convince them that we love each other very much and he assures them that he will stand by me no matter what happens, but my mum keeps goading him by pointing out how incompatible we are: school dropout vs school valedictorian, HDB flat vs Condominium apartment, blue-collar District 12 vs white-collar District 10 …

Adam keeps his cool, until she insists on calling his mum and insults her by reiterating how he isn't good enough for me, blaming him for ruining my life and berating her for not bringing him up properly. Before she can say anything about the baby, I stand up and rush over. "STOP IT!" I've had enough and I'm mortified by her irrational, snobbish and patronising behaviour. I grab the phone from my mum, apologise profusely to Adam's mum, hang up, grab Adam's hand and leave my home.

Bump and I are now homeless.

Interlude 8

As you join me on my journey, please take a musical break and listen to the song that captures the mood of that particular moment in time. Or read on.

The choice is yours.

'Papa Don't Preach', *song from the album 'True Blue'*
by Madonna, released June 1986

Consequences

"I CAN'T FACE your mum right now Adam. I'm so sorry for how my mum insulted her and I know I need to apologise for what happened, but I just need some time to think things through." We've been walking around for hours, our clothes plastered to skins slick with sweat and worry.

"It's getting dark, you need to eat something and rest" he urges. I'm grateful that he can't see my wry smile in the gathering gloom because food is certainly the last thing on my mind. I am eight months away from sitting my A-Level exams, Oxford entrance and Cambridge papers, and assuming I ace the exams, a year away from the glittering prize of reading Politics, Philosophy and Economics at Cambridge or English at Oxford, with one of the Ivy League universities as Plan B. I've been 'hothoused' over the course of my whole life for this ultimate purpose, only for our little vanilla bean seed to upset the apple cart, instantly derailing those carefully laid plans.

Sensing a seismic shift in our lives, Adam hugs me close to him, holds me tight and we place both our hands on my still-flat belly.

"Marry me" he whispers against my hair "Stop worrying, please. I love you both so much! I would do anything to make this work." We can feel our baby bean's presence and our love for him/her spills over so much that all I can taste is our salty tears as he kisses me tenderly with equal measures of longing and regret.

Surely love is enough. Please let me stay in this moment forever. I implore soundlessly to the Gods, my throat, lungs and heart join together as co-conspirators, twisting and constricting into a tight ball of hopeless anguish. *Please, please just let us be a family.*

We check into the cheap but clean motel in Chinatown with cash scraped together by digging deep in our pockets and rucksacks. This feels so shamefully seedy, but the hotel clerk doesn't even look at me as I grip Adam's arm like I'm on the downward leg of a rapid rollercoaster plunging into the unknown. The bed is as hard and unrelenting as my mother's ire, so sleep eludes me even though I'm emotionally exhausted. I run my fingers gently over Adam's shaved head while he sleeps, bemused at his ability to zonk out on command, grateful for the welcome distraction of the ceiling fan as it whooshes warm, stale air around this tiny shoebox of a room. Despite our dingy surroundings, I feel calmer than I've been all week. I feel supported and loved. I watch the blades swing languidly around in slow circles, inhaling and exhaling deeply to calm my nerves.

I'm running so fast that my hair is whipping into my face while the rain slams into my sponge-like body; I can feel the dank, dark dampness seeping into every pore as inch-by-inch, my cells fill up with water and my legs are engorged to the point of treacle-like solidity.

I. Struggle. To. Move. Any. Further… but I have to get going, I have to open all the gates to free all the elephants before they all drown to death. There are so many gates, all closing in on me in ever decreasing circles, looming over me and then contracting away as I reach for the locks. The harder I try, the less progress I make. I can hear the baby elephants trumpeting their distress and their mothers responding with a chorus of melancholy and helplessness. Everything is so waterlogged that I can't tell if it's the rain or my tears streaming down my face and cascading everywhere. I'm sinking, slowly but surely, the soporific stream seeping into my oxygen-deprived lungs, drowning in sorrow and shame. I feel myself spinning uncontrollably, like a mummy unravelling its bandages, spiralling downwards towards oblivion and eternal damnation …

"Simone, BREATHE! Simone, wake up! Oh God, don't leave me like this!" Adam's frantic cries and vice-like grip on my shoulders pull me out of the chasm towards the light. I wake to find the bedsheets drenched in sweat and tears, and we're both sobbing and clinging onto each other for dear life. My flippant fiend pipes up — *You should have just gone with it Simone. That was your get-out-of-jail-free card. The nightmare's only just begun.*

IT'S BARELY HALF past six on Monday morning when I finally persuade Adam to go home and make peace with his mum before returning to camp. I know she would be worried sick. I'm beginning to realise that being a parent is equal parts responsibility and fear, because any decisions I make can potentially mess up my baby's life. Feeling guilty about how I'd upset my parents, who must now be out of their minds with concern for my wellbeing, I head to the bus stop and get on the bus for Bukit Timah. I get off three stops before home and pause at the arched sign for Hwa Chong Junior College. It's make or break time, but there's still time to change course. *No there isn't*, Conscience reminds me, while Common Sense points out that our Principal starts his work day early when no one else is around, so I sneak into the admin building and knock timidly on his office door.

"Come in!" his voice booms cheerfully. "Oh hello Simone, er … why don't you take a seat over there …" He gestures to the chair opposite him, his voice trailing into a pregnant pause as he takes in my dishevelled, non-uniformed attire.

Eyes downcast, I pick at the worn fabric of my black jeans and explain my predicament. To his credit, he only flinches once when I declare rather defiantly how I've decided NOT to have an abortion.

"So I'm here today Sir, to ask if you can write to the PSC (Public Services Commission) and explain that due to ill health, I will be withdrawing my Oxbridge university applications."

"Have you taken leave of your senses, Simone? You're in the national top forty of your entire year group with a fully funded scholarship to the world's best universities, and you're going to throw away this once-in-a-lifetime opportunity? I think you should reconsider your decision. After all, as you say, you're probably less than a month in. There are question marks over whether a foetus can feel pain much before twenty-four weeks. You have at least twenty weeks to change your mind. Think about your parents if you're not bothered about yourself. What will your classmates think? Such a shame, girl. A crying shame."

I still my hands and rest them on my lap; stubbornly, I raise my chin and look him straight in the eye, "With all due respect sir, IT is NOT just a foetus. He or she is a baby, unborn as yet, but in my humble opinion, this baby is alive and sentient. Who are we to decide when life begins? In any case, you always talk to us about accountability. I accept that it was wrong to engage in pre-marital sex, but this is my mistake and I won't be able to live with myself if I make my baby pay for it with his or her life."

I can see him struggling to come up with a counter-argument. My Inner Conscience claps her hands and cheers me on as we sit in silence for what feels like an eternity, but is probably only a few minutes. Eventually, he sighs with resignation.

"You'll have to leave it with me, Simone. I need to talk to your parents as legally, you're still a minor. If you're really sure you want to do this, I will support you. But I have to warn you, as your Principal and also as a father to a teenage daughter of similar age to you, that this will be incredibly hard. In fact, I can't think of a single time a girl in your situation hasn't had an abortion. I know you love to be the first at everything Simone, but I advise you to re-consider."

"I understand sir. And I am grateful for your advice and concern. I know I won't change my mind whatever happens. I am in love with Adam and our baby has been created, rightly or wrongly, out of our love. We love him and want him to live his best life."

With tears pooling in my eyes, I stand, turn to go and pause at the door. Turning round, I leave him with one final thought, "After all, wasn't it Shakespeare who said that love is not self-seeking? What kind of parent would consider their own self before their child?"

It's nearly twilight by the time the Principal has had conversations with all relevant parties. I am still waiting in the 'isolation room' where naughty students go to serve detention. How ironic, I think — there's a first time for everything, even for a goody-two-shoes like me. My classmates think I am off sick and the Principal has been in and out all day sharing snippets of his perfect plan. A part of me sits in silent admiration at the slick unemotional efficiency of Operation Cover Up to Save Face — it's like a covert military exercise, all hushed tones and furtive glances. Another part of me knows that it's time to face the music, that I am alone. I resist the urge to run, kicking and screaming, out of this detention chamber, to run as fast and as far away as I can to the safety of anywhere-else-but-here. I feel sure that Adam's mum would welcome me with open arms if she knew, but my mind impatiently fast-forwards to four or five months hence in that cramped two-bed HDB flat, me waddling around like a beached whale getting under everyone's feet, my mum's disdainful words lingering like a prophetic sermon on repeat; Adam fed up with trying, and failing, to keep his family, me and our unborn baby happy, and us breaking up due to the wedge of resentment driven between us by too much happening too soon. Resigned and crestfallen, I pull my hand away from the door handle and plant myself back onto the stone-cold chair.

Ten minutes later, the Principal returns carrying a small sports bag I recognise as one of mine that I use when teaching aerobics in our college gym, accompanied by a nun who says nothing, but whose steely eyes tell me that she means business and will brook no argument. Ever.

"Simone, this is Sister Carmen. She's the supervisor at The Haven where you'll be staying until we decide what you're going to do. Your parents have been informed and they packed some of your belongings in this bag. They told me to tell you that ..." his voice trails into an uncomfortable pause as he struggles to find less hurtful words.

"That they think I'm crazy and they disown me?" I finish his sentence for him. The three of us stare wordlessly at each other while my words reverberate round the room with an air of finality.

"Er, well, um, they didn't quite say that," he stammers. With an exasperated sigh, he gives up but still tries to soften the blow, "Give them time, they'll come round eventually."

And just like that, twelve years of always being the high-achiever, the academic superstar, the one to watch because she is going places, come to an abrupt and underwhelming end.

#

THERE IS NO attempt at small talk during the taxi journey to The Haven. Sister Carmen is content to sit in stoic silence and I am too tired to care. My mind is preoccupied with a new game of Babyblip chess — I examine all possible outcomes with distant impartiality, as if this is happening to someone else. It's the only way I can cope with everything. Pretend this is happening to a close friend, stay logical, give sound advice to my friend and just keep going. Apparently sharks have to keep swimming even when sleeping or they die.

Do or die. The simplicity of these three words belies the complexity of real life.

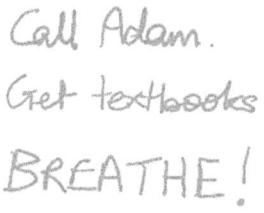

I rummage around in my sports bag for a pen and scribble my to-do list on the back of my hand. We're stuck in rush-hour traffic and the metronomic click of the taxi meter amplifies the disapproving judgement I see in Sister Carmen's pursed lips and rigid, uptight posture. I suspect girls like me are too far removed from her own life experience (having taken a vow of chastity) that it's probably hard for her to empathise. She must be impervious to all the sorry messes she witnesses, discharging her duty with perfunctory precision. When we get to the Thomson Road district, the heavens open in sympathy, the torrential rain, thunder and lightning mirroring my mood. Sister Carmen is not amused so I'm guessing we're close to our destination. Right on cue, the taxi pulls into the car park of a school set high on a hill. I get out and I'm drenched within seconds, while Sister Carmen stays resolutely dry under an umbrella she's miraculously pulled out from under her habit. She gestures for me to join her but doesn't wait for me to catch up, so I decide to embrace the tropical downpour — at least it makes me feel alive. I follow her down as she charges on ahead, around a towering bougainvillea bush peppered with pink blooms, surprised to see a dimly lit stone path behind a wrought iron gate that's concealed in between the bush and dense shrubbery. The stones are slippery from the storm, but Sister Carmen is sure-footed from familiarity and descends swiftly down the steps while I scrabble to keep up. I glimpse bursts of colour mushroomed in clusters on either side of the steps from the numerous tiny flowering plants clinging tenaciously onto the rocks and stony soil. I marvel at how life thrives in the most surprising and seemingly inhospitable circumstances; as Mama used to say to me, *where there's a will, there's a way.*

A minor commotion down below interrupts me mid-memory, Sister Carmen is speaking in harsh whispers to another nun but her voice carries because the storm is over as quickly as it began.

"This one's different so we have to put her in the vacant dorm until we know what to do with her."

The other (softer) voice protests, "But she'll be lonely and scared!"

"Hush! Don't be silly! She should be grateful to have a roof over her head after the trouble she's brought on her own family. Anyway, the other girls won't like her because unlike them, she can have an abortion but refuses to, so let's just isolate her till I've had another chance to talk to her parents, HCJC and the Church."

I clear my throat so they know I'm approaching. The nun next to Sister Carmen has the most smiley, kindest and warmest eyes I've ever seen, in a face as round and dimpled as a mooncake. She puts her arm around me and pulls me into the building, apparently oblivious to the rain dripping off me, pooling in puddles on the tiled foyer floor, and the waves of disapproval rolling off Sister Carmen like steam evaporating from a boiling kettle. I try my best to suppress a small, rebellious giggle.

"Hello dear, you must be tired and hungry. Let's get you out of these wet clothes first and then I'll warm up some noodles we had for dinner earlier. You must eat something before you go to bed. I'm Sister Claire but everyone just calls me Claire, so you can too."

"I'll leave you to it then, SISTER Claire!" Sister Carmen's peeved words linger as she ascends the stone steps briskly and disappears like an imagined apparition. I look at Sister Claire and we both burst out laughing.

#

Much as I hate to admit it, Sister Carmen was right about one thing: the other girls do not warm to me at all. After an uncomfortable night tossing and turning on my steel-sprung single bed, I brush my teeth and hair, splash cold water on my face in a vain attempt to revive myself, and wait for Sister Claire to collect me from the 'isolation' dorm at six in the morning. I help her prepare breakfast and set the table before the other 'inmates' arrive at 7am. Seven girls traipse into the dining/lounge area, all visibly pregnant and curious. They wait till Sister Claire has left for morning mass before quizzing me while we clear the table, wash and dry the dishes, then tidy the room. I answer all their questions as openly as possible, and soon gather from their responses that being pregnant is probably the only thing we have in common. I'm the youngest and still at school. Most of the others are in their early to mid-twenties and left school aged sixteen. All of them were abandoned by their boyfriends as soon as they found out they were pregnant. Five were unable to have an abortion because they found out they were pregnant after twenty-four weeks, while the other two could not have an abortion for medical reasons.

"So you're how many weeks now?"

"Only three or four lah, she already said so what!"

"Your boyfriend wants to marry you right? Aiyoh[66]! Why you so bodoh[67]?! Just marry him already lah!"

"For a smart girl, you're very gong-gong[68] one[69]."

Only one of them looks at me as if I'm not completely crazy. Turns out she's the oldest of us all, at twenty-nine. She takes me out into the garden to tend to the vegetables and plants while

---

66. Aiyoh: An exclamation of dismay or surprise.

67. Bodoh: Malay word meaning stupid.

68. Gong-Gong: Hokkien word meaning dumb (retarded).

69. One: A particle used at the end of a question or sentence to emphasise meaning.

the others disperse to do other chores within the house. She tells me that she foolishly fell in love with a married man who kept reassuring her that he would leave his wife for her, only to change his tune once she told him she was pregnant. Their clandestine affair has robbed her of most of her carefree twenties. Because she was clinging onto the hope that he would relent once he could see their baby growing, she left it till it was too late to have an abortion. Thankfully, her slim build and the way she carries her baby means she's been working right up to the last few months of her pregnancy. She's taken unpaid leave off work and used the money he gave her for a backstreet abortion to pay for living expenses. She will give her baby up for adoption, having already met the couple who will adopt him through some friends at work. They're rich, live in Indonesia and can give him a life that she can't, as a single mother whose strict Chinese parents would disown her if they even found out about the affair, let alone having a baby out of wedlock.

"Things would be so much simpler if I'd just gone for the abortion while I still could. Sometimes I really wish I had, then my life would be much better now. It's not been easy Simone. It won't be easy for you either. But honestly, don't bother about what the others say. Only you know what's best for you and your baby."

Oh what a tangled web we weave, when first we practice to deceive. I scoff ironically to my inner flippant fiend, as I revise for my English A-Level exam, which is imminent in a month's time. Sir Walter Scott must have been a prophet when he wrote 'Marmion', I think aloud, because I feel like he wrote that line about me. By now, my daily routine is programmed into autopilot and the other girls are used to my outcast status. I'm always up way past the 9pm lights-out curfew because, despite giving up my Oxbridge scholarship, I'm taking my A-Level exams as a private candidate, and have been teaching myself the curriculum for the past seven months. Sister Carmen and Sister Claire leave me alone in the isolation dorm to study by lamplight and no one bothers me as long as I'm awake by 6.30am every day to get on with my morning chores. The other girls resent that I have a lighter rota due to my revision schedule but frankly, I couldn't care less what they think. I know that some of them call my dorm 'the Shangri La' because I'm on my own and get to stay up late, but they have no idea what it's like to be inside your own head twenty-four-seven, or how the shadows in the deserted dorm assume morphed and misshapen forms, terrorising me on countless sleepless nights. Especially when I'm always alone.

In recent months, now that I can feel Bump move and sometimes even see a little arm or leg ripple under the skin of my abdomen as if to say *Hi mum, I'm here!*, I've begun talking to Bump to avoid having the same old boring conversations with Conscience, Common Sense or my darker Flippant Fiend. Even though I've had a few ultrasound scans, I chose not to find out Bump's gender but for some reason, I've begun to refer to Bump as he or him. Adam is convinced that Bump is a boy and has resolutely refused to look at girls' names. Instead we've decided to call him Marc. So almost every waking minute of every day, I converse with Marc. More recently, he responds with little kicks and moves his hands with amazing agility. We often play games when I'm lying alone in bed where I gently chase his hands and feet as he moves. Marc loves to hear me sing while I stroke his fingers – something that soothes him and sends us both to sleep every time. I pause my revision and describe to Marc the details of the tangled web we've been weaving over the last few months.

So Marc, your mama and grandpa refused to forgive me for quite a while. Mama kept calling me yah-bun[70] and a shameless hussy in letters and through Sister Carmen's messages. When you got bigger though, after Auntie Steph left to study Law at uni in London, they both decided to visit me every fortnight — sometimes to bring titbits but more often just to scold

---

70. Yah-bun: Stubborn in Hokkien.

me and remind me of the shame and scorn they will face if anyone finds out about 'the bastard child'! Auntie Steph sends me letters but we don't speak due to the time difference and international calling costs.

I talk to your daddy once a week but we only have short chats because Sister Carmen only allows each of us a few minutes to make outgoing calls. So I ring him on the public telephone in camp, where he's told his CO that his grandma is ill so he has to have regular phone calls every week for updates! It's also how we plan to get him some time out from camp when you're born. I'll call him to say his grandma has passed away and he'll be able to get a week off, fingers crossed.

I don't talk to any of my HCJC friends because our Principal decided to tell everyone that I've gone abroad to convalesce from chronic bronchitis. The last time I saw him was when he dropped off some exam prep documents at the top of the secret stairway, and stony-faced Sister Carmen delivered both the documents and his best wishes for my health in her usual dour tones. I honestly wonder why she does this job if she hates being around 'fallen girls' like us. That's what I heard her say about us girls at The Haven to Sister Claire the other day, that we are like fallen angels who have lost our way, along with our wings. She, your mama and grandpa keep pestering me for a decision on what I will do when you are born. She tells me that she's found a couple who want to adopt you and that I should seriously consider it. She knows I still want to study abroad and that your mama and grandpa hate your daddy. They all say that I've already given up enough and it's time to think about me. I honestly didn't know they cared!

I'm talking to your daddy about it this weekend when he comes to visit. I'm so excited to see him Marc, because the last time was nearly a month ago. Unfortunately, just as he left the visitors' bunker downstairs, he bumped into Mama and Grandpa because they were half an hour early. Mama chased him all the way down to the six-foot fence and he climbed over it in his hurry to get away from her because he couldn't wait for Sister Carmen to open the gate. I didn't know whether to laugh or cry, especially later that evening when one of the other girls bitched about the shouting and noise, then looked rather pointedly in my direction. I felt simultaneously embarrassed and mutinous — I really wanted to yell "Well, at least I get visitors!", but I didn't because it would have been really uncharitable and unkind!

But I digress. Your daddy and I have a very big decision to make this weekend. What should I do Marc? You are the reason why I'm here, and I have given up everything to give you your life. What should I do about you, my beautiful boy?

#

WHY DO I feel like I've been here before? The uneasy cloak of déjà vu lays heavy on my shoulders and around my dread-filled chest. Adam's jaw is set stubbornly and squarely as he stares out of the window in the mozzie-infested visitors' bunker at the encroaching tropical garden. Forty-five minutes have flown by and we are no closer to a decision. We're both however, close to tears and I can feel Marc's agitation as he thrashes wildly, signalling his vicarious distress. "How many more times do I have to say I love you and ask you to marry me before you accept it and just say yes? How many, Simone?"

"I know you love me and Marc, and I love you both more than life itself! As far as I'm concerned, we're already married." I gesture to the plain gold band on my ring finger. "But love isn't enough Adam. We won't get any help from my parents, they think you're the devil incarnate, your parents hate each other, there's no room at your family home and neither of us has a job or can get one. You haven't even told your mum about the mess we're in! Who's going to help us bring him up? Who's going to fight his corner when the other kids at school call him names and say nasty things to him and about us? And what happens to him when we turn into our parents, fall out of love, start having affairs and shatter all his dreams of true love. He'll end up exactly like us — children of broken homes, looking for love in books and music, becoming disillusioned about ever finding his soul mate. Is that what you want for our baby?"

Neither of us can see through our tears; I feel and share his anguish as we envision the harsh reality of what could be. Adam's at my side in a heartbeat, enveloping us in his warm, tight embrace. In that moment, we are family. Marc's movements return to normal, and we stay close-knit for the longest time. Until Adam reluctantly breaks the spell, bringing us back down to earth with a dull thud, "Tell Sister Carmen to go ahead with the adoption."

Just like that, our first and last decision as Marc's parents is made.

My mind concurs while my heart breaks.

Chaos

You take your first breath at 6.35am on 26 November 1987 after two hours of precipitated labour, basically two hours of unrelenting pain. You've surprised everyone, except me, by arriving ten days earlier than your due date of 5 December. When they place you on my chest, I wrap my arms around you and look into your trusting and innocent, yet knowing, eyes. I fall in love with you again. It's just you and me in this cold and clinical labour room; everyone else ceases to exist. For me — there is only you; you are the only one. Marc, you are the love of my life.

#

Twenty-four days earlier, on my eighteenth birthday, we'd been having one of our usual conversations, me rabbiting on about the first few exams I'd taken and making fun of the invigilator whose flushed face and averted eyes betrayed his discomfort and unease, and you responding with your usual vigorous movements and hand gestures. My exams are due to end before your due date, but I can't shake the premonition that you'll make a dramatic early entrance. I ask you if you're planning mischief and you kick to signal an emphatic yes!

Sister Carmen nearly has an apoplectic fit! She's so angry when I inform her of my decision to postpone my exams for a year that she's actually speechless with rage. I can understand her reaction and also your mama and grandpa's when they find out, but I just want to spend these last few weeks giving you my undivided attention.

#

It's too late to move me to the main dorm, but I am punished by a doubling of household chores on the rota. The day before your birth, as I dig deep into our vegetable patch to harvest carrots for dinner, my back starts to spasm and ache. The pain continues into the evening and night, but I'm fairly tolerant of pain and carry on regardless.

At 4.15am, I begin to feel an overwhelming sense of urgency, you're very active and I think I ought to wake Sister Claire, whose room lies in between Shangri La and the main dorm. I wait until I hear her door creak open at 5am, then call out to her before she goes out to attend morning prayers. Her face turns ashen when she sees me and she immediately unlocks the office door to call for a taxi. I plead with her to let me call your Daddy; thankfully, she says yes, so I make the hurried phone call to camp to say his grandma has passed away (code for 'Marc is on his way'). I ask Sister Claire to call my parents as I make my way down the stairs to the main road where Sister Carmen is waiting impatiently at the now-open wrought iron gate. My progress is slow because I have to stop every thirty seconds, doubling up in pain and trying to catch my breath. I travel alone to Mount Alvernia Hospital, where I was born eighteen years and twenty-four days before you. It's all a bit of a blur.

It's a traumatic delivery. There is no soothing water birth, relaxing pipe music or supportive partner by my side coaching me on how to breathe or massaging my back. Just a bevy of nurses who don't look much older than me, crowding around us as I lie on what feels like a cold steel altar, my legs strapped up in metal stirrups like a sacrificial lamb. By the time the gynaecologist arrives, I am ready to push, but you refuse to budge. Your heart rate monitor starts to beep furiously, telling everyone who will listen that you want to stay cocooned inside me, safe in our own haven away from prying eyes, wagging tongues and judgemental know-it-alls. The doctor calls for forceps and before I can protest, he makes the incision, plunges them in and pulls you out kicking and screaming. You don't stop your indignant screaming until they lay you on my chest, where I kiss and stroke your perfect face and perfect fingers, whispering sweet nothings into your ear while I marvel at just how perfect you are. You move your head to nuzzle into my neck like the missing piece of a jigsaw puzzle that is now complete.

You scream when they remove you, their reassurances falling on deaf ears, for I am just as anxious as you. I am inconsolable until they bring you, still screaming, to my room half an hour later. You hush as soon as I pick you up, cradling you to my chest, your soft-skinned face pressed against my left breast, so our hearts beat together as one. I'm still holding you when your daddy arrives. I see him pause at the door, overcome with emotion, our resolve to give you up for adoption wavering fast. Wordlessly, he makes his way over to hold us both tightly in his arms, our tears mingling with protective pride, pure joy and immeasurable sadness.

"Get away from her, you bastard!" Your mama's angry outburst shatters the peace with her machine-gun staccato snarl. Your daddy steps back but I can see his balled fists tense and flex with frustration where they lie motionless at his sides. Your grandpa wanders over and peeks at you, while your mama plucks you from my arms and holds you at arms' length, her features softening from furrowed frown to small smile. You remain calm but look bemused at all the scrutiny and attention. Your eyes are wide open and you start to angle your face from side to side; I instinctively feel the urge to hold you to my breast but right on cue, a nurse appears at the door holding out a bottle. Your daddy hands the bottle to me and your mama relinquishes you reluctantly. Everyone falls into an uncomfortable silence while I feed you; I deliberately zone out so it's just you and me, baby. For now.

It hurts to blink. It hurts to breathe. The nurses have been feeding me paracetamol throughout the day, but nothing numbs the searing pain I feel from top to toe. I hear your daddy anxiously asking for someone to call the doctor, but the nurses dismiss his concerns in the same way as they would swat away annoying flies. "Aiyoh! She's just young and can't handle pain. The doctor will be back later tonight so he can check her then. He's busy right now lah."

A few hours later, I hear your mama and grandpa conferring in hushed concerned tones. Your daddy feels my forehead and recoils at the heat emanating in waves, his face grave with concern. It's now 10.30pm and finally, the doctor bustles into the room. He checks my pulse and takes my temperature. I pry an eye open to see the colour drain from his face. The room lights up as though it's Christmas and I hear an alarm sounding as medical staff pile in from all directions. Your daddy takes you from me and I hear you screaming in protest. I try to hold on to you, but I have no strength in my cotton wool limbs; all I can feel is pain engulfing every pore in my body. They lift me onto another cold steel gurney and wheel me off at pace, the sterile hospital air rushing over my face so quickly that I can only just about smell the acrid antiseptic stench of nearly dead bodies. The last thing I see is the glaring porthole lights of the emergency operating theatre, then the blessed black backdrop of relief as I go under.

I'm floating in starless space and all I can see around me is an all-consuming darkness. I hear your heartbeat and feel you fluttering inside me. I want to stay here with you forever Marc, where it's quiet and peaceful, with no one shouting or screaming. Just you and me. We'd miss your daddy but it's always just been the two of us. Let's just stay here in the dark forever.

Unfortunately, I wake to hear your mama remonstrating loudly with the medical team. "So her heart stopped while you were operating, and you had to resuscitate! And now you tell me that if you'd operated just half an hour later, she would have died! You're lucky she didn't because I would sue all of you for negligence! How come your nurses didn't call for you sooner? He (pointing at your daddy) told them hours ago that she was in agony."

"Mrs Choo, I'm very sorry. It's no excuse but your daughter handled the pain so well, the nurses thought it was just pain from the stitches. It wasn't until I checked her that I realised she was suffering sepsis from the retained placenta. We weren't expecting her to haemorrhage from the D&C either, but she'll be okay now. There was quite a bit of scarring from the internal haemorrhaging though, so we just have to hope her fallopian tubes can recover."

"Does this mean she won't be able to have children in the future?" asks your grandpa.

"We don't know, Mr Choo. Time will tell."

"Where's Marc?" I whisper, reaching out for your daddy's hand.

"He's in the nursery. We can bring him back in when your parents and boyfriend go. But only if you feel strong enough, young lady — you've given us all a bit of a scare!" Sometimes I think things might have been easier if I had just let the darkness absorb me, so as to avoid the drama and heartache that followed.

LATER THAT DAY, your mama and grandpa leave to change their clothes and get something to eat. I'm secretly pleased that I now have some precious time with you and your daddy before they return. We're lying on the large hospital bed, with you and me playing our favourite game of stroking your fingers. I know babies apparently don't smile till they're older and if they look like they're smiling, it's probably due to wind, but you are loving the game and showing us your sweet smile.

"Let's keep him," he says. "We can make it work, Simone. My dad is hardly ever at the flat and my mum can help look after him while you study. I'll get a job as soon as I finish my NS. He's my son and I want to watch him grow up. I'll tell my mum if you say yes."

"What about your sister Adam? She's only ten! How are we going to get on with five of us sleeping in two bedrooms and a sitting room with a new-born baby? And it wasn't so long ago that you were convinced I had cheated on you with Sam, when we broke up last year. You don't even like it when I talk to another guy — how will you cope with all that when we'll also have the stress of bringing Marc up?"

"I've already apologised for the way I behaved — I just get really scared you're going to leave me for someone better, someone your mum approves of, some rich Chinese guy with a foreign degree and bright future, not a penniless mongrel like me. I can't help being possessive about you, and now Marc. You're my family and you're everything I want. If you think we can't make it work at mine, how about we speak to your parents? I'll swallow my pride and try to patch things up with your mum."

I hesitate and start chess-boarding different outcomes to see if we can make this work. I am desperate to be your mum in every way — to look after you, watch you grow and help you develop. I want to nurse you at my breast rather than feed you by bottle, I want to watch you crawl, take your first step and build up to a run. I'm curious to know what your first word will be and to find out if you'll love books and music as much as me. I want to witness every single moment of your precious life and guide you on your journey. I want more than anything to just love you. Is that too much to ask for?

We're rudely interrupted by the nursing team, who tell us they need to remove the ten meters of medical gauze the doctors left in my pelvis overnight to soak up the blood haemorrhaged during the emergency operation. Your daddy picks you up and takes you over to the window, looking out at the late afternoon sun, ant-sized people and honking traffic. I endure the embarrassing intrusion as best as I can, anxious to hold you in my arms again. My breasts are engorged with milk that I'm not allowed to feed you with and I can feel hard knots forming where they shouldn't be. They give me some pills to stop lactation and more painkillers, then start checking my vitals. I endure the fuss and try to hurry them up because all I can think about is you. I can't wait to hold you in my arms again.

WE'RE GOING TO try to have an adult conversation, all four of us. For once, I'm hopeful that we can work things out amicably without any histrionics. The nurses just came to take you for your bath and health check; they were cooing over how handsome you are and what a heartbreaker you'll grow up to be. Your daddy's chest swells up with pride and I chuckle when he pipes up, "That's my boy!" Your grandpa is smiling too, full of male camaraderie. Your mama scoffs, but in a good way because she too has repeatedly said what a good-looking boy you are. They are all besotted with you. Maybe, just maybe, we can find a way to make this work. I'm hopeful. I take a deep breath and begin.

"So, Mum and Pa, we've been thinking about things and just want to run a few ideas past you. We're wondering if we can somehow find a way to bring Marc up ourselves, with your help and support of course. Adam, Marc and I could always stay in Toa Payoh with his family, and I can study here instead of the UK. That will save you lots of money as you'll only have to pay for Steph's education. Of course we'll get married, so you won't have to worry about the kaypohs[71]. I really think we can make things work. What are your thoughts?"

I twiddle and spin my ring nervously as I speak. Your mama

---

71. Kaypohs: Busybodies/Gossips in Hokkien.

frowns and tells me to stop fidgeting before launching into an angry tirade. "Why do you insist on wearing that cheap ring? It's not even real gold. Why are you so desperate that you let that bastard fuck your zee-bai for free! How can you believe him when he hasn't even told his parents? You never learn from your mistakes. You just gave away your virginity for nothing because that useless bastard made you promises he's not intending to keep. Now you want to give up your education and your future? You're so stupid! I can believe I gave birth to such a stupid girl! You make me sick!"

Your daddy leaps up out of his chair, so upset that he's shaking with barely controlled anger. "Don't speak to her like that! We love each other and I really want to marry her! It's fine, we don't need your help! I can look after them on my own!"

"Sa, stop it! We already talked about this earlier. Why do you have to start? Adam, calm down, there's no need to make any hasty decisions." Your grandpa tries his best to referee, but fails spectacularly. *Well, this is going well so far*, my flippant fiend pipes up. I notice how they've triangulated around my bed — your daddy's on my left, your mama is on my right by the window and your grandpa is in the middle, at the foot of the bed. A part of me tries to think of a mathematical way that can bring three diametrically opposed points together to meet in the middle and agree the best outcomes for you. Sadly, I can't.

"So Mone, Pa's talked to your mum this morning and I think I've worked out how we can keep Marc. She doesn't want you to get married or give up studying abroad. I know we originally insisted that you give him up for adoption, but your boy is so cute! You already know your mum miscarried your brothers, so there is no one to carry on our family name. We can take him to a wet nurse for a few months until things settle down, so there's no gossip and your reputation isn't ruined. Then I'll bring him home and say he's my son from an affair I had when travelling on business. I'll raise him as my own, and he'll be like the son I never had but always wanted. Adam, you can still see Simone but only at our house and we'll supervise every visit." He pauses, all pleased with his plan.

"Just so I understand, you're basically saying that Marc will grow up thinking that I'm his older sister?" Your grandpa nods to confirm.

"Over my dead body! He's my son and he'll carry my name! I'm not having this! Simone, you can't let them take my son away from me!"

"You don't get a say in this, you bastard! You ruined my daughter's life, took advantage of her, and now you want to drag her down to your level so she can live like a pauper. You're all talk and no action. Your words mean nothing because you've done nothing! What's your plan?"

She pauses for his reply and is met with stony silence, so she continues, "That's right, you have no plan! Your parents are low class and from what I've heard, they only live together because they can't afford not to. Your father fucks his mistress on the side, while your mum says nothing and looks after your sister. I'm not having my grandson grow up like that! If I have my way, I will cut you out of their lives completely because you're just bottom-dwelling scum!"

She throws her heavy handbag at him, and he looks as if he's going to lose it as they move towards each other. Your grandpa is panicking in the face of events escalating into physical confrontation. My flippant fiend is watching the drama unfold with glee. By now, I'm inconsolable and sobbing so hard I feel like my heart's going to leap out of my chest.

"What about Marc? He's not some prized possession that belongs to any of you! Have any of you even stopped to think about what's best for him?"

The door flings open as the doctor and a few nurses march into the room to investigate the cause of the commotion. He takes one look at me and commands them to leave.

"OUT! You need to go because you're upsetting her! She needs to rest and recover." He checks my vitals and decides to sedate me. As he leaves the room to get the medication, I catch a glimpse of your daddy, mama and grandpa glaring at each other from across the corridor. I can't hear her, but I can see your mama remonstrating with him angrily while your grandpa holds her back. Your daddy flips them the bird, then turns his back on them and walks towards the stairs. I get up and run after him. "Adam, stop! Adam, please come back. We can work things out. Please don't leave us."

With angry tears streaming down his face, he shakes his head and disappears. The nurses pull me back into the room. There's blood dripping everywhere.

"I'm sorry, I'm sorry, I'm sorry …" I repeat over and over again as they clean me up. I'm not even sure who I'm apologising to or what I'm apologising for. I'm just sorry.

Once again, I feel very much alone.

ROCKING YOU TO sleep in my arms while gazing out of the hospital windows at the starry night sky, I think about the Ursa Major (the Great Bear) and Ursa Minor (Lesser Bear) constellations, and I reflect on how insignificantly small we all are — mere microcosms — when you consider the sheer scale of the universe. I remember Mama telling me about the sacrifices she'd made to bring up her last surviving children and the legend of the rabbit who sacrificed herself to the Emperor of Heaven so her babies would live. I recall the countless Reader's Digest stories of mothers who gave their lives to save their babies. I can completely relate. I feel very protective of you, Marc. You're my little bear cub and I would willingly sacrifice all that I have and all that I am, just to ensure that you live a happy life. In this painful moment of epiphany, I realise that there's one final choice I need to make. One that will be extremely unpopular with everyone else, the hardest choice of all, but the right choice for you.

#

IN THE FINAL weeks before your birth, the Straits Times reached out to the Catholic Church because they were looking to interview an unmarried teenager who had chosen to go through with her pregnancy. The only person anyone could suggest was me, because all the other teenagers they had contacted chose to have abortions. To protect my anonymity, I agreed only to write an article, a love letter to my unborn child, rather than an interview. It was heavily edited before publication to remove content and sentiments deemed unsuitable for the average Straits Times reader. The abridged article was published today, 1 December 1987, the worst day of my life.

I write a note to go with the article and pack it with your belongings.

My dearest Marc,

Even though you've only been with us for five days, I feel like I've known you forever. It's taking all the strength I have, to let you go to your new home to live with your adoptive parents. They are able to give you the start you deserve and the care that you need. All I can give you is my love, and sadly, that just isn't enough.

All I want is for you to live a happy life, your best life. I want you to grow up in a stable and loving family home, to learn about the world and its rich history, read voraciously, immerse yourself in art and music, marvel at science and innovation, travel to nourish your soul, fall in love, learn how to succeed or fail, but fail fast and try again. I just want you to live.

If your parents ever decide to tell you that you're adopted, you'll want to know how you came to be. Your father and I both come from dysfunctional families. We met when I was thirteen and he was sixteen — he was the DJ at a party I attended and it was love at first sight. We love each other deeply and in all ways except legally, we are married. In order to give you your life, I've given up a Government scholarship, my freedom and now, my heart, but you are worth every sacrifice. I was desperate to be your mum and to be a close guide on your life's journey, but I didn't want you to grow up in a climate of lies, hate and shame, the odds stacked against you from the start. It's not fair on you and you deserve to be happy.

Know that you are wanted, that you are loved, that someone somewhere is always thinking of you, every minute of every day. I've been told that this is a closed adoption so I won't be able to watch you grow up. I promise to find you. Until then, I hope you are happy. I hope you find love. I hope we will meet again. I love you infinitely.

With all my love, always, your Mum
xxxxxxxxxxxxxxxxxxxxxxxxxx

I write a letter to your prospective adoptive parents asking them to give you my note and article, if they ever choose to reveal your background, so you will know that you are very much wanted and loved. I do all of this robotically, almost as if I am having some kind of out-of-body experience. Maybe it's the only way I can deal with the indescribable heartbreak I'm trying so hard to hold at bay.

Your mama is inconsolable because she is losing her beloved grandson. She screams at me as she leaves the visiting area of 'The Haven', "You're worse than an animal! Far, far worse because even a Mother Tiger would rather die than abandon her cubs." Her words slice through my already lacerated heart. I cry as I feed and change you, then rock you to sleep for the last time. I cry even more when the Sisters come for you and take you from me to begin your new life.

I cry still.

#

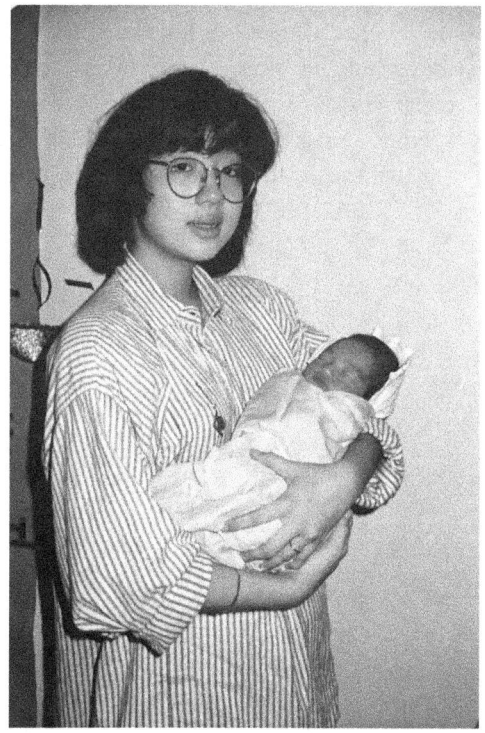

I've read somewhere that amputees can still feel pain where their amputated parts once were, and cardiologists believe that people can develop cardiomyopathy and even die from a broken heart. I know this to be true from the dark days following my final fateful decision and even writing this makes me feel like I lost you yesterday. Faced with my first choice eight months ago, I rather frivolously listed 'Preserve Figure' as a pro for abortion; ironically, I'm the slimmest I've ever been within a week from your birth.

I don't sleep. I barely eat. I sleepwalk my way through life, zombie-like, robotically going through the motions so everyone else will think I'm fine. I cry all the time, the cavernous void inside me filled to the brim and overflowing with all the unspoken words I used to whisper to you when you were nestled inside me. I miss you so, so much. Dying inside, little by little every day, and unable to stem the tide any longer, I surrender to the inevitable tsunami of depression, drowning in the depths of a despair so dark and desperate, so laden with regret, so full of the deepest longing for you, that I am lost, irrevocably and unequivocally, lost.

Interlude 9

As you join me on my journey, please take a musical break and listen to the song that captures the mood of that particular moment in time. Or read on.

The choice is yours.

'Stop Crying Your Heart Out', *song from the album 'Heathen Chemistry' by Oasis, released June 2002*

Postlude

(December 2022)

"Nothing I can do is going to bring them back."

Cristina Peck, 21 Grams, movie 2003

"You can search the entire universe and never find a being more worthy of love than yourself."

Donny, Isn't It Romantic, movie 2019

THIRTY-FIVE YEARS LATER, regret is my constant companion as I replay various alternate endings and recreate multiple what-if scenarios. Every year at 6.35am on 26 November, regardless of which time zone I'm living in, I wake up with that familiar feeling of loss and devastation, grieving your absence all over again. I wonder what you're doing, whether you're looking at the stars when I am and wondering about me too. I wonder what music you listen to, if you're happy, whether you have children. I wonder. I feel like there are two Me's — the one the world sees, a high-functioning depressive, and eighteen-year-old Me who still longs for you every minute of every day.

For over a decade afterwards, I remember how I couldn't walk past a Mothercare shop without bursting into tears, or even buy baby clothes as gifts for close friends experiencing the joy of becoming first-time mums; how I couldn't hold a new-born baby without the heavy weight of grief and loss knotting together to form a hard lump constricted in my chest. Ever since your birth, I've not been able to see the light without noticing the shadows.

Every few years, I go back to Singapore to visit your mama and grandpa. I ask Sister Carmen how you're doing, and she says you're growing well. When you turn eighteen, I ask the new sisters in charge at The Haven if it's possible to contact your adoptive parents for more details, but they stonewall me. With the advent of the internet, I spend hours trawling through various search engines but am hampered by having no knowledge of your adopted surname. All I have is the first name I gave you and your date of birth.

I promise to keep searching for you until the day I die because I know you will need answers. I know you will feel abandoned even if you read my letter and the article I wrote for the Straits Times. I know you will feel like you weren't lovable enough for me to keep you. I know you will be angry with me for leaving you. I know you need closure as much as I do. I just want to hold you again, tell you how sorry I am and how much I still love you, wholly, unconditionally.

It took over twelve years for me to feel I was in the right head space to have another child. I'm glad I waited, because I think it would have been extremely unfair on my children to have a mum who wasn't emotionally available and present. As soon as your brother and sister are able to understand, I tell them about you, how much you mean to me and the heartbreakingly hard decisions I made when I was seventeen and eighteen. We remain hopeful that I will find you one day. Someday soon, hopefully.

I don't know who said that life is not a bed of roses, because my life has taught me that it is. Rose bushes have thorns as a defensive mechanism to ward off predators and prevent long-lasting damage. I believe that life *is* a bed of roses — to truly live life to its fullest, you have to embrace the pleasure with the pain. I will never stop reaching for the roses regardless of how many thorns I may encounter along the way. I just need to get better at spotting the thorns, choosing the best route around them, and pausing to look after any wounds inflicted by the thorns I can't avoid, making sure they heal before I move on. Start, stop, start again.

I know I should have stopped to deal with your loss. I realise now that my sense of self-worth was so low, I began to make choices that would sabotage my own happiness. For example, staying in abusive or unfulfilling relationships because of my perverse desire for self-punishment, and the belief that I didn't deserve anything good or wholesome. Even though my head believed I had made the right choices, my heart was less forgiving. *You deserve nothing more than misery*, drummed my heart's silent mantra, always taunting, seeking retribution for the hurt I had caused her. I used to think that being strong was all about suffering in silence. It's taken years of self-reflection to realise that the bravest word in the whole world that anyone can ever utter is…

HELP

The truth is, being strong isn't about putting on a brave face, pretending that everything is okay and soldiering on. Being strong is about admitting our fears and voicing our vulnerabilities, asking for other kind souls to treat us as we deserve to be treated. It's about choosing to surround yourself with compassionate people who help you to shine, to walk away from the darkness. Being strong is about treating ourselves as we treat others — with empathy, compassion and care. With love.

I've learned the hard way that you can't serve from an empty jug. It is finally time to stop running on empty. Once again, I'm faced with another life-defining choice — step into the light and focus on forgiving and healing myself, or succumb to and be consumed by the ever-present darkness of self-doubt and low self-esteem. So, I choose love and happiness. And I'll start by being kind.

To me.

END OF BOOK ONE

Watch this space for The Fate We Make | Book Two: Hurting

Acknowledgements

I AM GRATEFUL for:

- My parents who always tried their best. It would be easy to blame them for saddling me with generational baggage, but they're only human. Like all of us.
- Cate Caruth, for being my content alchemist and for challenging me to provide more context following your thorough reader review.
- Chris Newton, for your empathetic and brilliant copy editing and for taking the time to listen.
- Ken Dawson, for your patience and creativity. I love the book cover and how you went the extra mile to enhance my photos and illustrations.
- Kate Coe, for your meticulous typesetting, book design and 'polishing'.
- Pete Hoare, for printing and delivering the limited edition for launch.
- Gilly Lee and Greg Stephenson of Perry Road Studios and Lewis Peters, for recording and producing the audiobook.
- Anthony Harvison and Captain Jon Kirk at Palamedes, for outstanding PR.

- ♥ Kristen O'Connell, for your marketing magic.
- ♥ Aimee, Laura and the BookMachine team for your brilliant handling of the launch event.
- ♥ Mun, aka mrbrown, for writing the foreword and for your non-judgemental friendship.
- ♥ Mavis, for your unwavering support and faith in me, without which I would never have dared to share my story.
- ♥ Viv and Kevin, for reading early drafts and providing invaluable feedback.
- ♥ Phil, Rich, Nikki, Seema, Andy, Ryan, Joo Shin and my Embrace ERG friends at Microsoft, for being more than just colleagues. You inspire me to bring my best every day.
- ♥ Deli, for bringing music and light into my life.
- ♥ Hils, for making me laugh through the tears.
- ♥ Lesley, for reminding me to be kind to myself.
- ♥ My drinking buddies at the Bridge House in St Neots, past and present, for making it easy to be myself and for the banter.
- ♥ Joe and Samaria, for being my 'why'. For your unconditional love and groundedness.
- ♥ Doug, my Prince Charming, for loving me just the way I am. For always making me feel that I am enough. For being my guiding light, best friend and tower of strength.

Thank you all from the bottom of my heart.

About the Author

SIMONE WARREN ESCAPED the confines of Singaporean society by travelling, first through reading books from the age of six, then by studying, living and working abroad for over thirty years. Her love of people and psychology has seen her succeed as a senior executive working for global technology providers including Alibaba and Microsoft. Her career is a far cry from her roots in literature, drama and music, as lead actor in stage plays and President of the Creative Writing Society at university. Today, she is rediscovering her dream of becoming a great storyteller. She lives in Cambridgeshire, UK, with Prince Charming and two grown-up children who are far more sensible than their parents.

www.ingramcontent.com/pod-product-compliance
Lightning Source LLC
Chambersburg PA
CBHW071226080526
44587CB00013BA/1517